WHERE TO GO AND WHAT TO DO ON LONG ISLAND

Third Revised Edition

by SCOPE
(Suffolk County Organization for the Promotion of Education)

DOVER PUBLICATIONS, INC.
Mineola, New York

Bibliographical Note

Where to Go and What to Do on Long Island, first published in 2002, is the third revised edition of the work first published by Dover Publications, Inc., New York, in 1993. Willard L. Hogeboom, consultant.

Library of Congress Cataloging-in-Publication Data

Where to go and what to do on Long Island / by SCOPE (Suffolk County Organization for the Promotion of Education). — 3rd rev. ed.
     p.   cm.
  Includes indexes.
  ISBN 0-486-42479-0 (pbk.)
  1. Long Island (N.Y.)—Guidebooks. 2. New York Region—Guidebooks. I. Suffolk County Organization for the Promotion of Education (Suffolk County, N.Y.)

F127.L8 W54 2002
917.47'210444—dc21
                               2002025721
                                CIP

Manufactured in the United States of America
Dover Publications, Inc., 31 East 2nd Street, Mineola, N.Y. 11501

CONTENTS

NASSAU COUNTY

Contents / *v*

SUFFOLK COUNTY

Contents / *xi*

MAP REFERENCE

NASSAU COUNTY

1. Albertson
2. Baldwin
3. Bayville
4. Brookville
5. Cold Spring Harbor
6. East Norwich
7. East Rockaway
8. Elmont
9. Franklin Square
10. Freeport
11. Garden City
12. Glen Cove
13. Hempstead
14. Hicksville
15. Jones Beach
16. Kings Point
17. Lawrence
18. Long Beach
19. Lynbrook
20. Manhasset
21. Massapequa
22. Mineola
23. New Hyde Park
24. Oceanside
25. Old Bethpage
26. Old Westbury
27. Oyster Bay
28. Plainview
29. Port Washington
30. Rockville Centre
31. Roslyn and Roslyn Harbor
32. Sea Cliff
33. Seaford
34. Syosset
35. Uniondale
36. Wantagh
37. Westbury

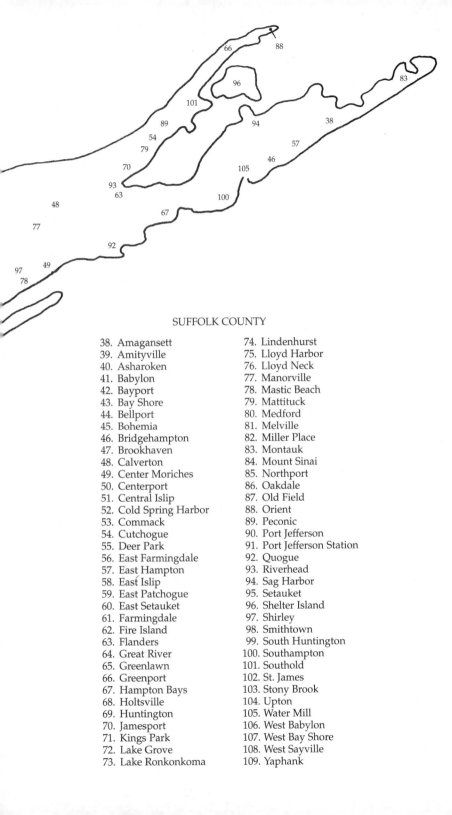

SUFFOLK COUNTY

38. Amagansett
39. Amityville
40. Asharoken
41. Babylon
42. Bayport
43. Bay Shore
44. Bellport
45. Bohemia
46. Bridgehampton
47. Brookhaven
48. Calverton
49. Center Moriches
50. Centerport
51. Central Islip
52. Cold Spring Harbor
53. Commack
54. Cutchogue
55. Deer Park
56. East Farmingdale
57. East Hampton
58. East Islip
59. East Patchogue
60. East Setauket
61. Farmingdale
62. Fire Island
63. Flanders
64. Great River
65. Greenlawn
66. Greenport
67. Hampton Bays
68. Holtsville
69. Huntington
70. Jamesport
71. Kings Park
72. Lake Grove
73. Lake Ronkonkoma

74. Lindenhurst
75. Lloyd Harbor
76. Lloyd Neck
77. Manorville
78. Mastic Beach
79. Mattituck
80. Medford
81. Melville
82. Miller Place
83. Montauk
84. Mount Sinai
85. Northport
86. Oakdale
87. Old Field
88. Orient
89. Peconic
90. Port Jefferson
91. Port Jefferson Station
92. Quogue
93. Riverhead
94. Sag Harbor
95. Setauket
96. Shelter Island
97. Shirley
98. Smithtown
99. South Huntington
100. Southampton
101. Southold
102. St. James
103. Stony Brook
104. Upton
105. Water Mill
106. West Babylon
107. West Bay Shore
108. West Sayville
109. Yaphank

INTRODUCTION

E VEN IF YOU HAVE LIVED a lifetime on Long Island, exploring its highways and back roads, you will find this a book of revelation—of places you never knew existed and things you never knew before.

For the casual visitor or vacationer, city dwellers looking for a change of pace, teachers and group leaders planning field trips, sportsmen, students, nature lovers, history buffs, sun worshippers, families, adventurous senior citizens and singles—in fact, for anyone looking for fun, excitement or pleasurable learning—these pages open the door to a treasure trove of places to go and things to do. Here you will find information on visiting parks, museums, historic buildings, recreational facilities, communications centers, businesses, industries, nature and science centers and government and public service institutions.

Make your Sunday outing or your vacation trip more meaningful by planning to stop off at one or several of the many places of interest to be found along your route. Keep this book handy as a reference to the sights of Long Island and its culture, history, resources and natural beauty. Take young people out into the world that surrounds Long Island schools with invaluable educational experiences. The information on each site includes a recommendation as to appropriateness for various grade levels, facilities available and charges, if any. Teachers will discover many possibilities: going to hospitals for health education, to Walt Whitman's birthplace in connection with poetry or to Home Sweet Home in connection with music.

All information about places of interest contained in this book has been carefully checked and updated. If changes occur, for instance in telephone numbers, revised information can be obtained from websites, telephone directories, Chambers of

Commerce or local governments. Also, note that the word "to" as in "June to September" should be understood as meaning "to and including." The book is divided into two sections, Nassau County and Suffolk County, and is alphabetized first by municipality, then by institution within a given municipality.

NASSAU COUNTY

Clark Botanic Garden of the Town of North Hempstead

CLARK BOTANIC GARDEN occupies 12 rolling acres in Albertson, adjacent to the Albertson LIRR Station, in central Nassau County. The aim of the Garden is to convey the beauty, fascination and importance of the plant world. Horticultural and landscape features include three ponds, a canopy of mature white pines, extensive woody plantings, a rose garden, an herb garden, a daylily garden, a wildflower garden, an iris garden, an early-flowering garden, a rock garden, a dwarf conifer garden, perennials and annuals. Programs are for adults and children, registered individually or in groups. Subject areas include gardening, botany, nature and the environment. Clark Botanic Garden is a living catalog of landscape ideas for the home gardener.

Address/Telephone	193 I.U. Willets Road Albertson, NY 11507 (516) 484-8600
Website	www.clarkbotanic.org
When to Visit	Monday to Sunday 10:00 a.m. to 4:30 p.m. (No admittance after 4:00 p.m.) Call for possible holiday closings Groups by appointment
Charges/Fees	None
Suggested Grades	4–Adult
Guided Tour	Yes, by special arrangement
Maximum Group	60

1

Group Notice	2 weeks
Eating Facilities	Picnic area
Restroom Facilities	Yes
Handicapped Access	No
Additional Information	Special programs are offered for children in grades 4–6 and for adults. Off-site programs are available in North Hempstead. Special events include plant sales, music concerts, a Halloween Spooky Walk, Earth Day celebration, a late-summer Seniors Day and a Fall Festival. Clark Botanic Garden is a Division of the Town of North Hempstead Parks & Recreation Department.

Baldwin Historical Museum

HOUSED IN ITS headquarters built for the bicentennial, the Baldwin Historical Society's young but growing museum contains photographs, artifacts and memorabilia from Baldwin's past.

Address/Telephone	1980 Grand Avenue Baldwin, NY 11510 (516) 223-6900
When to Visit	Wednesday and Sunday—1:00 p.m. to 3:00 p.m., and by appointment
Charges/Fees	None
Suggested Grades	3–Adult
Guided Tour	Yes, 30 minutes, by appointment.
Maximum Group	30
Group Notice	3 weeks
Eating Facilities	None
Restroom Facilities	Yes
Handicapped Access	No
Additional Information	Slide presentations available. Single floor access for handicapped.

Bayville Historical Museum

THE BAYVILLE HISTORICAL Museum, established in 1972, is located in the North wing of the Bayville Village Hall complex. The Museum, owned and operated by the Incorporated Village of Bayville, is dedicated to the people of Bayville for the collection, preservation and interpretation of memorabilia of historical value to this village. The exhibits include: Victorian furnishings, vintage clothing and accessories; Bayville School classroom with memorabilia dating from 1851; a room dedicated to the late Mona and Harrison Williams with photos of their Bayville estate, known as "Oak Point"; a room with exhibits of agricultural tools of the past; a room dedicated to Bayville's Flower Shellfish Industry; a room devoted to Bayville's "O.H. Perry" General Store memorabilia; research files and an extensive collection of photographs; and special seasonal exhibits each winter and spring.

Address/Telephone	34 School Street
	Bayville, NY 11709
	(516) 628-1720 or (516) 628-1439
When to Visit	Tuesday and Sunday—1:00 p.m. to 3:00 p.m.
	By appointment for school and other groups
	Closed during July, August and holidays
Charges/Fees	None
Suggested Grades	4–Adult
Guided Tour	Yes
Maximum Group	28 children with 4 *attentive* adults
	No maximum for adult groups
Group Notice	2 weeks minimum
Eating Facilities	None
Restroom Facilities	Yes
Handicapped Access	First floor only

Hillwood Art Museum
(C. W. Post Campus of Long Island University)

H ILLWOOD ART MUSEUM, located on the C. W. Post Campus of Long Island University in Brookville, N.Y., presents a year-round schedule of temporary and permanent exhibitions that cover topics from antiquity to the cutting edge of contemporary art. The 4,500-square-foot Museum boasts a beautiful curved gallery which Phyllis Braff of the *New York Times* has called ". . . one of the Island's most dramatic showcases for art. . . ." Hillwood Art Museum's impressive and eclectic Permanent Collection consists of objects dating from the earliest of man's creative endeavors to contemporary art. The Museum conducts an active and well-attended Education Program that includes Family Day activities, a Tuesday Evening Lecture and Performance Series, and extensive hands-on educational programs for local schools.

Address/Telephone	720 Northern Boulevard Brookville, NY 11548 (516) 299-4073
Website	www.liu.edu/museum
When to Visit	Monday, Wednesday, Thursday and Friday 9:30 a.m. to 4:30 p.m. Tuesday—9:30 a.m. to 7:30 p.m. Saturday—11:00 a.m. to 3:00 p.m.
Charges/Fees	None
Suggested Grades	3–Adult
Guided Tour	By appointment. Hands-on Education Program for Visiting Schools as well as docent-style tours.
Maximum Group	30 students, no limit on adults
Group Notice	Call for information.
Eating Facilities	Yes
Restroom Facilities	Yes
Handicapped Access	Yes
Additional Information	Free, ample, accessible parking.

Tilles Center for the Performing Arts
(C. W. Post Campus of Long Island University)

THERE ARE FEW halls in the nation with the acoustics, sightlines and performing space to match the excellence of this concert theater. Concerts, lectures and other cultural events with world-famous performers take place throughout the year.

Address/Telephone	Northern Boulevard
	Brookville, NY 11548
	(516) 299-3100
Website	www. tillescenter.org
When to Visit	Write or call for most recent schedule
Charges/Fees	Varies with program
Suggested Grades	K–Adult, depending on program
Guided Tour	None
Maximum Group	Unlimited
Group Notice	Depends on program
Eating Facilities	Yes, by arrangement
Restroom Facilities	Yes
Handicapped Access	Yes
Additional Information	Subscriptions available, contact box office. Infrared hearing assistance system.

Cold Spring Harbor Fish Hatchery and Aquarium

THIS HATCHERY WAS established in 1883 by New York State. Visitors will see New York State's largest collection of native freshwater fish, reptiles and amphibians, housed in 40 aquariums, indoor and outdoor turtle habitats, a 20-foot indoor stream exhibit and an amphibian display. Fish in the six outdoor ponds may be seen in various stages of their growth cycle. There are three buildings on the site: The Walter Ross Aquarium Building, the Fairchild Exhibit Building and the Hatch House. The hatchery is located on the south side of Route 25A, just west of the Nassau-Suffolk border.

Address/Telephone	*Route 25A (west of Nassau-Suffolk border) Cold Spring Harbor, NY 11724 (516) 692-6768
Website	www.cshfha.org
When to Visit	Daily 10:00 a.m. to 5:00 p.m. Closed Easter Sunday, Christmas and Thanksgiving days
Charges/Fees	Adults—$3.50; children (5–17) and seniors (over 65)—$1.75; children under 5 and members—free Programs: $3.00 per person/1-hour program; other programs available.
Suggested Grades	All ages
Guided Tour	Organized groups and schools call for arrangements
Maximum Group	20–25, with a maximum of three groups at one time depending upon program
Group Notice	Call for reservation as soon as possible
Eating Facilities	Picnic tables only
Restroom Facilities	Yes
Handicapped Access	Yes
Additional Information	Visitors may feed the fish. Call for information on special programs. *Mailing address: P.O. Box 535, Cold Spring Harbor, NY 11724

Muttontown Preserve

THIS 500-ACRE PRESERVE was set aside to protect Nassau County's dwindling natural habitats. Both marked and unmarked trails are found throughout the preserve. Topographical features typical of the north shore, such as glacially formed rolling hills, are in evidence, along with kettle hole ponds, meadow and woodland. Trail maps, guided nature programs, cross-country ski trails and equestrian trails are available.

Address/Telephone Muttontown Lane
East Norwich, NY 11732
(516) 571-8500

When to Visit Daily
Groups—Monday to Friday
9:30 a.m. to 4:30 p.m.

Charges/Fees Public—Free
$35.00 per 1½ hour program
$45.00 per 2 hour program

Suggested Grades K–Adult

Guided Tour Yes, 1½ hours; also 2 hours

Maximum Group 3 classes with a maximum of 30 students each

Group Notice 2 weeks

Eating Facilities None

Restroom Facilities Yes

Handicapped Access Yes

Additional Information Absolutely no collecting of plants or animals. Stay on trails. Operated by Nassau County Department of Recreation and Parks.

Old Grist Mill Museum

L OCATED IN THE OLDEST building in Nassau County, this one-time grist mill is now home to a museum. In addition to the milling area, exhibits include a barber shop, dental office, general store, bay life, an 1894 Fire Pumper and Indian area. The museum is unique because all artifacts are from old East Rockaway families. A scale model of East Rockaway, c. 1900, is also on display. Recovered and restored from fire in 1990, the museum welcomes visitors.

Address/Telephone Woods and Atlantic Avenues
East Rockaway, NY 11518
(516) 887-6300

When to Visit	Saturday and Sunday
	First weekend in June until Labor Day
	1:00 p.m. to 5:00 p.m.
	Groups by appointment
Charges/Fees	None
Suggested Grades	K–Adult
Guided Tour	Upon request
Maximum Group	Unlimited
Group Notice	None
Eating Facilities	None
Restroom Facilities	None
Handicapped Access	Yes

Breakfast at Belmont

WHILE EATING BREAKFAST in the trackside café, you can relax and watch the horses breeze through their morning workouts on the racing oval. NYRA commentators are on hand to share Belmont history and present interviews with jockeys, trainers and other racing personalities. When visiting the Paddock, track personnel will demonstrate the techniques and equipment used in grooming, training and riding. A tour of the Backstretch will give visitors a view of the starting gate and barn area.

Address/Telephone	*Belmont Racetrack
	Hempstead Avenue
	Elmont, NY 11003
	(718) 641-4700, ext. 4494
Website	www.nyra.com
When to Visit	Daily except Mondays and Tuesdays
	Racing days for breakfast: May 8 to July 21 and
	September 6 to September 29
	Saturday, Sunday and holidays (not available on
	Belmont Stakes Day)
	7:00 a.m. to 9:30 p.m.
	Call for exact dates and events

Charges/Fees	Parking and admission
	Breakfast at reasonable prices
Suggested Grades	K–Adult
Guided Tour	Yes, 30 minutes
Maximum Group	60, with adequate supervision
Group Notice	1 week
Eating Facilities	Yes
Restroom Facilities	Yes
Handicapped Access	Yes
Additional Information	*Mailing address: Customer Service Dept., N.Y. Racing Association, P.O. Box 90, Jamaica, NY 11417

The Nassau Pops Symphony Orchestra

THE REPERTOIRE OF The Nassau Pops Symphony Orchestra is devoted exclusively to the performance of popular and light classical music. Based in the Village of Mineola, the orchestra presents a full summer concert series in many of the parks in Nassau County. In addition, they provide the pit orchestra for annual Long Island park tours of fully staged Broadway shows presented in conjunction with Plaza Productions. Since 1989, The Nassau Pops has presented a Fall performance at Tilles Center for the benefit of Special Olympics on Long Island, and has raised tens of thousands of dollars in donations for this charity through ticket sales to these concerts. The orchestra's season ends in December with two Christmas performances, one at St. John's University, and one at Corpus Christi Church in Mineola.

Address/Telephone	859 Willow Road
	Franklin Square, NY 11010
	(516) 565-0646
	Fax: (516) 486-2362
	Email: info@npso.org
Website	www.npso.org
When to Visit	June to December

Charges/Fees	Summer park performances are free. Provide your own seating. Call for information on fall and winter performances.
Suggested Grades	K–Adult
Guided Tour	None
Maximum Group	According to location
Group Notice	Write or call for information
Eating Facilities	None
Restroom Facilities	According to location
Handicapped Access	According to location
Additional Information	Receive a free subscription to The Nassau Pops Symphony Orchestra newsletter of upcoming events by sending or emailing your name and address.

Freeport Historical Society Museum

THIS MUSEUM SPECIALIZES in local heritage. Emphasis is placed on the evolution of the local histories of Freeport and the surrounding villages, the vaudeville era and shipwrecks along the nearby coast.

Address/Telephone	350 South Main Street Freeport, NY 11520 (516) 623-9632
Website	www.freeporthistory.org
When to Visit	May to December Sundays—2:00 p.m. to 5:00 p.m.
Charges/Fees	Donation
Suggested Grades	3–Adult

Guided Tour	Yes, 1 hour for schools and groups by appointment
Maximum Group	25
Group Notice	3 weeks
Eating Facilities	None
Restroom Facilities	Yes
Handicapped Access	No

Cradle of Aviation Museum

H OUSED IN TWO 1932 hangars and a spectacular new building at the former Mitchel Air Force Base, the Museum portrays the aerospace heritage of Long Island. Thus far, over sixty aircraft and spacecraft, mostly built on Long Island, have been collected. The Museum has been renovated into a world-class air/space museum, including an advanced large-screen Omnimax theatre, and a space-themed restaurant.

Address/Telephone	Mitchel Field
	Garden City, NY 11530
	(516) 572-4111
When to Visit	Open daily
Charges/Fees	Varies with program
Suggested Grades	K–Adult
Guided Tour	None
Group Notice	2 weeks
Eating Facilities	Yes
Restroom Facilities	Yes
Handicapped Access	Yes
Additional Information	Call for schedule, events and theatre showtimes.

Firehouse Gallery
(Nassau Community College)

V ISITORS WILL SEE art exhibits featuring painting, sculpture, crafts, prints, drawings and photography. These change monthly. There are also lectures, demonstrations and speakers each month. The gallery also sponsors competitions in the various art mediums.

Address/Telephone	Nassau Community College Garden City, NY 11530 (516) 572-7165 Fax: (516) 572-7302
When to Visit	Monday, Tuesday, Thursday, Friday and Saturday—11:00 a.m. to 4:00 p.m. Wednesday—11:00 a.m. to 7:00 p.m. Closed Sunday
Charges/Fees	None
Suggested Grades	3–Adult
Guided Tour	None
Maximum Group	50, with one adult per group of 25
Group Notice	Call in advance
Eating Facilities	Yes, nearby
Restroom Facilities	Yes
Handicapped Access	Yes

Long Island Children's Museum

T HE LONG ISLAND Children's Museum is a learning laboratory where hands-on exhibits invite visitors to experiment, examine and play. Through lively interdisciplinary activities, children and adults can share in the excitement of the learning process as they explore the world in which we live. Exhibits include: *Communication Station, Bubbles, TotSpot, Bricks & Sticks, Music, Changes & Challenges, ClimbIt@licm, Pattern Studio, Tool Box,*

Sandy Island, and *KaleidoZone.* Changing special events on weekends include multicultural performances, crafts and in-depth exploration of exciting topics.

Address/Telephone	11 Davis Avenue Garden City, NY 11530 (516) 224-5800
Website	www.licm.org
When to Visit	Wednesday to Sunday—10:00 a.m. to 5:00 p.m. Closed Monday and Tuesday
Charges/Fees	$8.00 per person
Suggested Grades	K–6; Programs for infants to age 12 available.
Guided Tour	Yes
Maximum Group	75
Group Notice	Reservations required at least 2 months in advance
Eating Facilities	Yes
Restroom Facilities	Yes
Handicapped Access	Yes

Garvies Point Museum and Preserve

THE CENTERPIECE OF a 62-acre preserve overlooking Long Island Sound, the museum specializes in the archaeology and geology of the area. Five miles of nature trails offer a diversified look at the natural surroundings and habitat of the north shore of Long Island. Changing exhibits from seashells to minerals to dugout canoes inform and educate visitors about the natural heritage of the land.

Address/Telephone	Barry Drive Glen Cove, NY 11542 (516) 571-8010

When to Visit Preserve: 8:30 a.m. to dusk
Closed Mondays
Museum hours: Tuesday to Saturday
10:00 a.m. to 4:00 p.m.
Sunday—10:00 a.m. to 4:00 p.m.
Groups by appointment Tuesday to Friday

Charges/Fees Adults—$2.00
Children—$1.00
Educational program—$45.00 (plus $1.00 per
student)

Suggested Grades K–Adult

Guided Tour Museum education program groups by
appointment

Maximum Group 30, with one adult per group of 10

Group Notice 3 weeks

Eating Facilities Picnic facilities nearby

Restroom Facilities Yes

Handicapped Access Yes

Additional Information No collecting, digging or cliff climbing. Educational
programs rain or shine; dress appropriately.
Operated by the Nassau County Department of
Recreation and Parks.

Holocaust Memorial & Educational Center
of Nassau County

THE HOLOCAUST CENTER of Nassau County is a unique resource that
seeks to bridge the gaps between the tragedy of the past, the comfort
of the present, and the hope of the future. Through lectures, seminars and
special events, the Holocaust Center fosters a greater understanding of the
causes and consequences of one of the darkest periods in world history.

Address/Telephone Welwyn Preserve
100 Crescent Beach Road
Glen Cove, NY 11542
(516) 571-8040
Fax: (516) 571-8041

Website www.holocaust-nassau.org

When to Visit Monday to Friday
9:30 a.m. to 4:30 p.m.
Sunday—11:00 a.m. to 4:00 p.m.
Closed Saturdays

Charges/Fees None

Suggested Grades 5–Adult

Guided Tour Yes, provided for minimum of 10 people—
By reservation only

Maximum Group Call for information

Group Notice 4 weeks

Eating Facilities None

Restroom Facilities Yes

Handicapped Access Yes

Additional Information Reservations taken for school and organization
group tours.

Welwyn Preserve

THIS 200-ACRE nature preserve bordering on Long Island Sound has on its grounds a field ecology study station that provides prime examples of a mixed deciduous forest, a stream valley, a freshwater pond, a salt marsh and a beach.

Address/Telephone Crescent Beach Road
Glen Cove, NY 11542
Preserve: (516) 571-8500
Holocaust Center: (516) 571-8040

When to Visit	Monday to Sunday Open all year 9:30 a.m. to 4:30 p.m.
Charges/Fees	Visit free.
Guided Tour	None
Eating Facilities	"Brown bag"
Restroom Facilities	No
Handicapped Access	No
Additional Information	Holocaust Memorial Center is located on the grounds. Preserve is operated by the Nassau County Department of Recreation and Parks.

Hofstra Museum
(Hofstra University)

THE HOFSTRA MUSEUM includes three dedicated indoor exhibition spaces: the Emily Lowe Gallery; the David Filderman Gallery, 9th floor, Axinn Library; the Rochelle and Irwin A. Lowenfeld Conference and Exhibition Hall, 10th floor, Axinn Library; and the outdoor sculpture on Hofstra's north and south campus areas. The Museum's permanent collection of more than 4,000 objects contains major works of art, specializing in modern European and American painting, sculpture, photographs and prints as well as Asian, Oceanic, African and pre-Columbian art. The Museum is responsible for more than 50 pieces of outdoor sculpture in various locations throughout the 240-acre campus. Walking tour maps can be found in the galleries. The Museum coordinates about 16 exhibitions annually and occasionally features special lectures and accompanying programs.

Address/Telephone	Hofstra Museum Emily Lowe Gallery 112 Hofstra University Hempstead, NY 11549 (516) 463-5672 (office phone, Mon.–Fri: 9–5 p.m.) (516) 463-7446 (recorded information)
Website	www.hofstra.edu/museum

When to Visit	Tuesday to Friday—10:00 a.m. to 5:00 p.m.
	Saturday and Sunday—1:00 p.m. to 5:00 p.m.
	Closed Mondays and holidays
	Summer hours: Monday to
	Thursday—10:00 a.m. to 5:00 p.m.
	Closed Fridays, holidays and weekends during
	June and July
Charges/Fees	Free admission
Suggested Grades	1–Adult
Guided Tour	Self-guided tour
Maximum Group	15 (children should be accompanied by at least
	2 adults)
Group Notice	2 weeks
Eating Facilities	Yes, campus cafeteria
Restroom Facilities	Available on campus
Handicapped Access	Yes

The Hicksville Gregory Museum
(Long Island Earth Science Center)

THE HICKSVILLE GREGORY MUSEUM, with the largest mineral collection on Long Island, features over 4,000 specimens of rocks and minerals, including fluorescent displays, shells and gems. Located in the original Heitz Place Court House, a national historic site, the museum also displays changing historic exhibits. The Old Court House Jail, one of the few "Old Town Lock-ups" still surviving, is open to the inspection of curious visitors.

Address/Telephone	Heitz Place & Bay Avenue
	Hicksville, NY 11801
	(516) 822-7505
	Fax: (516) 822-3227
	Email: gregorymuseum@earthlink.net
Website	www.gregorymuseum.org

When to Visit	Monday by appointment Tuesday to Friday—9:30 a.m. to 4:30 p.m. Saturday and Sunday—1:00 p.m. to 5:00 p.m. Closed Thanksgiving, Christmas, New Year's Day
Charges/Fees	Adults—$5.00; senior citizens and children—$3.00 Schools and groups: Students (tour included)— $5.00 Children under 5, members and Hicksville residents free
Suggested Grades	K–Adult
Guided Tour	Yes, 1 to 2 hours
Maximum Group	50, with one adult per group of 10
Group Notice	1 month minimum
Eating Facilities	None
Restroom Facilities	Yes
Handicapped Access	Yes
Additional Information	Slide and lecture programs available.

L. I. Reptile Museum

THE MAIN OBJECTIVE of the L. I. Reptile Museum is to make education come alive by transporting children and adults into the world of the Rain Forest, the Desert, or the Savannah. The museum has two floors filled with thousands of live, exotic reptiles and amphibians, living in state-of-the-art museum quality exhibits, depicting their natural environment. Have a hands-on experience with some of our most gentle creatures in the large petting area, supervised by our experienced reptile keepers. See exciting live shows, including live venomous shows on the weekends.

Address/Telephone	70 Broadway Hicksville, NY 11801 (516) REPTILE, (516) 931-1500 Fax: (516) 931-1554
Website	www.reptilemuseum.com

When to Visit Daily—10:00 a.m. to 6:00 p.m.
Friday—10:00 a.m. to 8:00 p.m.
Closed Thanksgiving, Christmas, New Year's Day

Charges/Fees Adults—$9.95; children—$7.95; children under
3—free. Please call for school and group rates.

Suggested Grades Pre-K–Adult

Guided Tour Yes, for schools, camps, groups or parties.
Outreach programs available upon request.

Maximum Group 450

Group Notice 1 day

Eating Facilities Yes, Snake Bites Cafe

Restroom Facilities Yes

Handicapped Access Limited

Additional Information Reptique Boutique Gift Shop
Pet Shop—Live reptiles and supplies

American Merchant Marine Museum

SITUATED IN THE historic, turn-of-the-century Gold Coast estate once owned by William Barstow, the American Merchant Marine Museum is a wonderful place to visit. Home of the National Maritime Hall of Fame and the Sperry Navigation Wing, the Museum's extensive collection of ship models, painting, prints, documents and maritime artifacts emphasize the Museum's theme "Ships Made America."

Address/Telephone United States Merchant Marine Academy
Kings Point, NY 11024
(516) 773-5515

Website www.usmma.edu

When to Visit Tuesday to Friday
10:00 a.m. to 3:30 p.m.
Saturday and Sunday
1:00 p.m. to 4:30 p.m.
Groups: Monday to Friday, by appointment
Closed federal holidays and the month of July

American Merchant Marine Museum

JOHN KASIUS

Charges/Fees	Donation
Suggested Grades	3–Adult Teachers should call for special school packet
Guided Tour	Yes, for groups by appointment—can be combined with a tour of the U.S. Merchant Marine Academy
Maximum Group	30
Group Notice	1 month
Eating Facilities	Picnic facilities
Restroom Facilities	Yes
Handicapped Access	Yes

United States Merchant Marine Academy

THIS ACADEMY WAS founded in 1943 to prepare young men and women as officers for the American merchant marine and for leadership positions in the maritime industry. Visitors will observe midshipmen training for various careers within the industry. Points of interest on campus include the Mariners Chapel and the American Merchant Marine Museum.

Address/Telephone	Kings Point, NY 11024
	(516) 773-5387 Call: Office of External Affairs
When to Visit	Open all year except July and federal holidays
Charges/Fees	None
Suggested Grades	K–Adult
Guided Tour	Yes, 1 hour (for groups only)
Maximum Group	40
Group Notice	2 weeks
Eating Facilities	Seafarer Restaurant
Restroom Facilities	Yes
Handicapped Access	Limited
Additional Information	Speakers available for high schools only.
	Ship's stores open Monday to Friday—8:00 a.m. to 4:00 p.m.

Rock Hall Museum

ONE OF THE finest pre-Revolutionary War houses on Long Island, Rock Hall was completed in 1768 by Josiah Martin, a wealthy West Indian plantation owner. Constructed of wood in the Georgian style then prevailing for fine British homes, the two-and-a-half-story house was home to only two families (the Martins and the Hewletts) before being deeded to the Town of Hempstead for museum purposes in 1948. Today, the magnificent white mansion contains a Federal-period dining room, parlors, a reconstructed warming kitchen, and authentic bedchambers that offer a splendid glimpse of well-to-do life on Long Island spanning more than two centuries.

Address/Telephone	199 Broadway
	Lawrence, NY 11559
	(516) 239-1157
When to Visit	Open year-round
	Wednesday to Saturday—10:00 a.m. to 4:00 p.m.
	Sunday—Noon to 4:00 p.m.
	Closed Monday, Tuesday, and major holidays
Charges/Fees	None
Suggested Grades	K–Adult
Guided Tour	Yes, approximately 1 hour and 15 minutes
Maximum Group	30 (one adult per group of 10 children)
Group Notice	Call for appointment
Eating Facilities	Yes, picnic facilities
Restroom Facilities	Yes
Handicapped Access	No

Long Beach

A SOUTH SHORE WATERFRONT resort and residential community with a wide sandy beach and boardwalk open to the public. The City of Long Beach is known for its wide variety of ethnic restaurants.

Address/Telephone	City of Long Beach
	Office of Public Relations
	1 West Chester Street
	Long Beach, NY 11561
	(516) 431-1000, x309
Website	www.longbeachny.org
When to Visit	Daily
	Lifeguards on duty 8:30 a.m. to 6:00 p.m.
	Beach officially opens June 28
Charges/Fees	Adults—$6.00; children under 13—free
	Free parking (though not plentiful)
Guided Tour	None

Maximum Group	Unlimited
Group Notice	None
Eating Facilities	Boardwalk with concession stands
Restroom Facilities	Yes
Handicapped Access	Yes (Surf Chairs)
Additional Information	Directions to Long Beach (barrier island): Follow Meadowbrook Causeway, Atlantic Beach Bridge or Long Beach Bridge to Pacific Boulevard to Ohio Avenue.

Long Beach Medical Center

L ONG BEACH MEDICAL Center is a 403-bed medical center, teaching hospital, rehabilitation center and skilled care nursing home. State of the art diagnostic, medical and surgical procedures performed here are comparable to large hospitals. Virtually every medical service except obstetrics and every surgical procedure except open heart surgery and organ transplants are performed at this facility.

Address/Telephone	455 E. Bay Drive Long Beach, NY 11561 (516) 897-1095—Community Relations
Website	www.lbmc.org
When to Visit	By appointment
Charges/Fees	None
Suggested Grades	K–Adult
Guided Tour	Yes, 1 hour
Maximum Group	25
Group Notice	2 weeks
Eating Facilities	None
Restroom Facilities	Yes
Handicapped Access	Yes
Additional Information	Call in advance with information relative to group ages, focus of interest, etc.

Fantasy Playhouse
(Theater Workshop)

F ANTASY PLAYHOUSE PRODUCES original musicals based on children's classics featuring students of the Playhouse's theater school as well as some Broadway revivals using professional actors. The Playhouse is open all year with classes for children, teens and adults and performances geared to all age groups. It also brings shows to schools, camps and libraries.

Address/Telephone	48 Atlantic Avenue Lynbrook, NY 11563 (516) 599-1982
Website	www.theaterworkshop.org
When to Visit	Call or write for schedule
Charges/Fees	Call or write for information
Suggested Grades	K–Adult
Guided Tour	Magic of Theater—$8.00 per person
Maximum Group	250
Group Notice	2 weeks
Eating Facilities	Refreshment stand
Restroom Facilities	Yes
Handicapped Access	Yes
Additional Information	Theater programs presented at your school—musical/drama/comedy—by arrangement

The Science Museum of Long Island

T HE SCIENCE MUSEUM of Long Island is a science education activity center. It was formed to stimulate children's interest in science and provide them with opportunities to participate in the excitement of discovery, to involve the adult public in the world of science and to expand the community's interest in our natural environment.

Address/Telephone	1526 N. Plandome Road Manhasset, NY 11030 (516) 627-9400

When to Visit	Monday to Friday and weekends by reservation only
Charges/Fees	Varies by program
Suggested Grades	Pre-K–Adult
Guided Tour	None
Maximum Group	Varies by program
Group Notice	By reservation only
Eating Facilities	Indoor lunchroom and outdoor picnic facilities
Restroom Facilities	Yes
Handicapped Access	Yes

John F. Kennedy Wildlife Sanctuary

THIS AQUATIC-ORIENTED outdoor wildlife area is located on over 500 acres of tidal marshlands. One can hike along an old road to any of several blinds.

Address/Telephone	*Tobay Beach Massapequa, NY 11758 (516) 797-4114
When to Visit	Memorial Day to Labor Day—4:30 p.m. to dark Winter—8:00 a.m. to dark Permit required (no charge)—Applications available at address below
Charges/Fees	None
Suggested Grades	3–Adult
Guided Tour	None
Maximum Group	Unlimited
Group Notice	1 month
Eating Facilities	None
Restroom Facilities	Yes, nearby
Handicapped Access	No
Additional Information	*Mailing address: c/o Town of Oyster Bay, Dept. of Parks, 977 Hicksville Rd., Massapequa, NY 11758

Old Grace Church Historic Complex
(Historical Society of the Massapequas)

OLD GRACE CHURCH, the oldest church in Massapequa, was erected by members of the Floyd-Jones family in 1844. The church, with its stained glass windows, offers an excellent example of church architecture of the period. A c. 1880 house located on the church grounds offers an excellent example of a working-class house of the period. The Delancey Floyd Jones Library is on site.

Address/Telephone	*4755 Cedar Shore Drive and Merrick Road Massapequa, NY 11758 (516) 799-2023
Website	www.massapequahistory.org
When to Visit	Sunday, May to September 2:00 p.m. to 4:00 p.m. Open to public. Groups by appointment.
Charges/Fees	None
Suggested Grades	4–Adult
Guided Tour	Yes, 1 hour, 1½ hour, and 2 hour by request.
Maximum Group	50
Group Notice	By reservation
Eating Facilities	None
Restroom Facilities	Yes
Handicapped Access	No
Additional Information	Parking lot. Historic Floyd-Jones Cemetery in rear. *Mailing address: P.O. Box 211, Massapequa, NY 11758

Nassau County Courts

THIS TRIP OFFERS students a special lecture on the criminal justice system and a tour of a New York State Supreme Court. The tour includes an introductory movie on the evolution of the jury system, an introduction to the jury system, and a question and answer period with a New York State

Court Officer. If the court schedule permits, an opportunity will be afforded to witness an actual Supreme Court trial and students may speak with a Supreme Court Justice. Also included is a tour of the Supreme Court Detention Facility.

Address/Telephone	Office of Community Relations
	100 Supreme Court Drive
	Mineola, NY 11501
	(516) 571-1478
When to Visit	By appointment only
Charges/Fees	None
Suggested Grades	Age 14–Adult
Guided Tour	Yes, 2 hours for orientation and observation
Maximum Group	35
Group Notice	Make arrangements as early as possible
Eating Facilities	Yes, cafeteria
Restroom Facilities	Yes
Handicapped Access	Yes
Additional Information	Speakers available to schools.
	To attend special demonstration trials write to: Dan Bagnuola, Director of Community Relations, N.Y. State Supreme Court, Mineola, NY 11501

Nassau County Executive/Legislature

THE NASSAU COUNTY Ralph G. Caso Executive and Legislative building houses the executive and legislative branches of Nassau County government. The County Executive seat and the 19-member Legislature were created in 1996 to replace a six-member Board of Supervisors and to better represent the County's 1.4 million residents. The County Executive oversees the administration of the County's various agencies and departments, whereas the Legislature makes local laws and possesses certain oversight powers.

Address/Telephone	Nassau County Ralph G. Caso Executive Building
	One West Street
	Mineola, NY 11501
	(516) 571-3131
When to Visit	By appointment
Charges/Fees	None
Suggested Grades	9–Adult
Guided Tour	Yes
Maximum Group	30
Group Notice	2 weeks
Eating Facilities	No
Restroom Facilities	Yes
Handicapped Access	Yes
Additional Information	The County Legislature meets biweekly on Mondays. For times and dates contact the Clerk of the Legislature at (516) 571-4253.

Nassau County Police Department

DEPENDING ON THE age and interests of the group, the visit can include a film on police operations and a walk through the 911 Emergency Communications Center, police museum and central testing unit. Other tours include the Mounted Unit and Children's Safety Town.

Address/Telephone	1490 Franklin Avenue
	Mineola, NY 11501
	(516) 573-7135
When to Visit	Tuesday to Thursday
	10:00 a.m. to 1:00 p.m.
Charges/Fees	None
Suggested Grades	7th grade–Adult
Guided Tour	Yes, 1 hour
Maximum Group	25, with adequate supervision
Group Notice	1 month
Eating Facilities	None
Restroom Facilities	Yes

Handicapped Access Yes

Additional Information Special classroom programs available. For tours of
local police precincts in Nassau County, contact
the commanding officer of the individual precinct.

Nassau County Police Museum

THIS MUSEUM SERVES as a repository of artifacts collected during the 70+
years of the Nassau County Police Department's service to the public.
Exhibits include a 1925 Harley Davidson motorcycle with sidecar and a
stationhouse scene from the early days. Also on display are confiscated
weapons, laboratory equipment, badges, air and marine gear and many
photographs depicting Department activity since 1925.

Nassau County Police Museum

Address/Telephone	Police Headquarters
	1490 Franklin Avenue
	Mineola, NY 11501
	(516) 573-7620
When to Visit	Call for hours.
Charges/Fees	None
Suggested Grades	3rd grade–Adult
Guided Tour	By appointment: Call (516) 573-7620
Maximum Group	30
Group Notice	1 month
Eating Facilities	None
Restroom Facilities	Yes, nearby
Handicapped Access	Yes

Eglevsky Ballet

T HE EGLEVSKY BALLET is nationally known for elegant, compact versions of the great classics, as well as an impressive sampling of neoclassical and contemporary ballets. Performing locally and across the country in major theaters and community venues, the company has appeared before more than 1,000,000 viewers. In addition, The Eglevsky Ballet offers an annual summer workshop for the serious ballet student and a year-round professional training program.

In addition to the celebrated production of *The Nutcracker,* presented annually at the Tilles Center, recent productions include: *Romeo and Juliet* excerpts, Tchaikovsky waltzes, and mixed repertory pieces at St. Joseph's College, Patchogue, N.Y., Steppingstone Park, Great Neck, N.Y., and Schreiber Auditorium, Port Washington, N.Y. New works are scheduled to be premiered in the coming year. Please call for information.

Address/Telephone	999 Herricks Road
	New Hyde Park, NY 11040
	(516) 746-1115
	Fax: (516) 746-1117
Website	www.eglevskyballet.com

When to Visit	Call to be placed on the mailing list and for specific program information.
Charges/Fees	Varies with program
Suggested Grades	K–Adult, depending on program
Guided Tour	Select programs only
Maximum Group	2,200
Group Notice	Varies with program
Eating Facilities	None
Restroom Facilities	Yes
Handicapped Access	Yes

Goudreau Museum of Mathematics in Art and Science (The Math Museum)

THIS ONE-ROOM museum and ancillary classroom space is bursting with puzzles, colorful geometric sculptures and math games. The "Math Museum's" message is that math is fun. A variety of activities and programs proves that message to be true. The museum features hands-on learning experiences for all ages.

Address/Telephone	Herricks Community Center 999 Herricks Road (Rm. 202) New Hyde Park, NY 11040-1353 (516) 747-0777
Website	www.mathmuseum.org
When to Visit	Monday to Saturday General public and groups by appointment only Several Saturdays of each month—open house October to May—Noon to 3:00 p.m.
Charges/Fees	$2.00 per person
Suggested Grades	K–Adult

Guided Tour	Variety of programs (most 2 hours)—call for additional information
Maximum Group	Up to 70, depending on types and ages of students
Group Notice	As much notice as possible
Eating Facilities	None
Restroom Facilities	Yes
Handicapped Access	Yes
Additional Information	Teachers are encouraged to bring cameras. Special programs done off-site for schools and groups. Enrichment programs offered on Saturdays. Additional programs offered during school vacations.

Marine Nature Study Area
(Town of Hempstead)

THE MARINE NATURE Study Area is a 52-acre preserve devoted to environmental education and natural history. To complement the outdoor features, there is an interpretive center that contains tanks with live specimens of marine life from the area and informative displays. Objectives of such an area include: an outdoor laboratory for elementary and secondary schools, salt marsh ecology, marine conservation practices, earth science, marine biology, and nature study. The Area also provides opportunity for research in marsh ecology and management to local college students and opportunity for art and photographic studies.

Address/Telephone	500 Slice Drive Oceanside, NY 11572 (516) 766-1580
Website	www.michael.farina.com/OMNS.htm
When to Visit	Tuesday to Saturday—9:00 a.m. to 5:00 p.m. Closed on holidays
Charges/Fees	None
Suggested Grades	3–Adult
Guided Tour	Reservations are required

Maximum Group	50
Group Notice	At least 2 weeks in advance
Eating Facilities	Pair of picnic tables
Restroom Facilities	Yes, but *not* handicapped accessible
Handicapped Access	Trails system, yes; restrooms, no

Cultural Arts Playhouse

THE CULTURAL ARTS PLAYHOUSE is a 260-seat fully equipped, three-quarter-round playhouse specializing in fully staged musicals, children's theatre, educational theatre, touring theatre and special events. Typical productions include *Jekyll & Hyde, Kiss of the Spiderwoman, The Scarlet Pimpernel, Crazy For You, 42nd Street,* and more. Open to the public and operating year-round. We have a musical theater and acting academy available to grades 1 through 12 with classes seven days a week. Educational theatre is available to school groups throughout the school year. Children's theatre is available on Saturdays and select Sundays. Mainstage theatre available Friday through Sunday. Schools and groups call for rates and schedules.

Address/Telephone	714 Old Bethpage Rd.
	Old Bethpage, NY 11804
	(516) 694-3330
	Fax: (516) 694-3343
Website	www.culturalartsplayhouse.com
When to Visit	Box Office Hours:
	Wednesday—3:00 p.m. to 6:00 p.m.
	Thursday—Noon to 6:00 p.m.
	Friday—11:00 a.m. to 8:30 p.m.
	Saturday—11:00 a.m. to 8:00 p.m.
	Sunday—11:00 a.m. to 4:00 p.m.
Charges/Fees	Mainstage tickets: $18.00 ($2.00 discount for seniors and students)
	Children's theatre: $8.00
Suggested Grades	Pre-K–Adult

Guided Tour	None
Maximum Group	260
Group Notice	1 to 2 months
Eating Facilities	Yes, concession area
Restroom Facilities	Yes
Handicapped Access	Yes
Additional Information	Birthday parties available with children's theatre.

Nassau County Fire Service Academy

T HIS SERVICE ACADEMY is a specialized school in fire fighting where Nassau County volunteer firefighters receive the latest and most scientific instruction in fire fighting and fire prevention. Visitors will see fire fighting techniques in action.

Address/Telephone	300 Winding Road Old Bethpage, NY 11804 (516) 572-8600
When to Visit	Monday to Thursday May to October 7:30 p.m. to 9:30 p.m.
Charges/Fees	None
Suggested Grades	K–7
Guided Tour	Yes, 30 minutes
Maximum Group	30, with adequate supervision
Group Notice	1 month
Eating Facilities	None
Restroom Facilities	Yes
Handicapped Access	No
Additional Information	Most local fire departments offer tours and fire prevention programs.

Old Bethpage Village Restoration

Old Bethpage Village Restoration

T HIS RESTORATION REPRESENTS a living-history museum that depicts farm and town life on Long Island in the mid-19th century, with over 55 historic structures on site. The rural community includes a hat shop, a schoolhouse, an inn, a general store, several farmhouses, farm animals and other reminders of a way of life typical of old Long Island. The authentic homes and furnishings, as well as the active craftspeople, farmers and housewives all in period clothing, recreate the lifestyle of a bygone era.

Address/Telephone 1303 Round Swamp Road
Old Bethpage, NY 11804
(516) 572-8400
Group reservations: (516) 572-8408

When to Visit March to May:
Wednesday to Friday—10:00 a.m. to 4:00 p.m.
Saturday—10:00 a.m. to 5:00 p.m.
Sunday—Noon to 5:00 p.m.
May to October:
Wednesday to Sunday—10:00 a.m. to 5:00 p.m.
November and December:
Wednesday to Saturday—10:00 a.m. to 4:00 p.m.
Sunday—Noon to 4:00 p.m.
Open Memorial Day, Fourth of July, Labor Day and
Columbus Day. Closed January and February.

Charges/Fees Adults—$6.00; Children—$4.00; children under
5—free. Call for group rates.

Suggested Grades K–Adult

Guided Tour 2-hour self-guided tour

Maximum Group 25, with adequate supervision for each class

Group Notice 1 month

Eating Facilities Yes; picnic area and cafeteria

Restroom Facilities Yes

Handicapped Access Yes; Reception Center and five historic buildings

Additional Information Appropriate attire for outdoors and walking on dirt
paths. Operated by the Nassau County Depart-
ment of Recreation, Parks and Support Services.

New York Institute of Technology
(Fine Arts Department)

THE FINE ARTS Department features gallery exhibits in the areas of
sculpture, photography, painting and graphics. These changing
exhibits feature the work of talented faculty members, students and artists
from outside the campus community.

Address/Telephone New York Institute of Technology
268 Wheatly Road
Old Westbury, NY 11568
(516) 686-7542 Call: Fine Arts Dept.

When to Visit	Monday to Friday
	September to June
	9:00 a.m. to 5:00 p.m.
Charges/Fees	None
Suggested Grades	6–Adult
Guided Tour	None
Maximum Group	Unlimited
Group Notice	None
Eating Facilities	Yes, cafeterias on campus
Restroom Facilities	Yes
Handicapped Access	Yes

New York Institute of Technology
(Tours of Laboratories)

VISITORS WILL BE taken on a tour of the computer science laboratory, which offers some of the latest and most sophisticated systems available.

Address/Telephone	New York Institute of Technology
	268 Wheatly Road
	Old Westbury, NY 11568
	(516) 686-7828 Call: Mechanical Engineering Dept.
When to Visit	Monday to Friday
	September to May
	9:00 a.m. to 5:00 p.m.
Charges/Fees	None
Suggested Grades	8–Adult
Guided Tour	Yes, up to 2 hours in length
Maximum Group	20, with 1 adult per group of 10
Group Notice	3 weeks
Eating Facilities	Yes, cafeteria
Restroom Facilities	Yes
Handicapped Access	Yes

New York Institute of Technology
(Tour of Radio and Television Studios)

THIS TRAINING FACILITY contains 2 color television studios, a video editing laboratory, a television newsroom, UPI wire service and state-of-the-art equipment in all areas. Also on premises are three radio laboratories equipped with modern stereo and mono consoles. A sound processing laboratory has voice recording and sound transfer and mixing facilities, including an 8-channel mixing board.

Address/Telephone	New York Institute of Technology
	268 Wheatly Road
	Old Westbury, NY 11568
	(516) 686-7567 Call: Communication Arts Dept.
When to Visit	Monday to Friday
	September to June
	9:00 a.m. to 4:30 p.m.
Charges/Fees	None
Suggested Grades	8–Adult
Guided Tour	Yes, 1 hour
Maximum Group	20, with one adult per group of 10
Group Notice	2 weeks
Eating Facilities	Yes, cafeteria
Restroom Facilities	Yes
Handicapped Access	Yes

Old Westbury Gardens

CONSTRUCTED IN THE style of an 18th-century English country estate, Old Westbury Gardens offers the visitor a view of the grandeur associated with Long Island, complete with a furnished mansion surrounded by formal gardens, open lawns, ponds, lakes and woodlands.

Address/Telephone	71 Old Westbury Road Old Westbury, NY 11568 (516) 333-0048
Website	www.oldwestburygardens.org
When to Visit	Wednesday to Monday Late April to mid-December 10:00 a.m. to 5:00 p.m.
Charges/Fees	General admission—$10.00; seniors (62+)—$8.00; children—$5.00 Group rates: 20 or more by arrangement
Suggested Grades	K–Adult
Guided Tour	Yes, house and garden, 2 hours
Maximum Group	120
Group Notice	4 weeks
Eating Facilities	Picnic facilities and outdoor café
Restroom Facilities	Yes
Handicapped Access	Yes
Additional Information	Call for information regarding educational tours.

Old Westbury Gardens

Coe Hall

Coe Hall
(At Planting Fields Arboretum State Historic Park)

THE TUDOR-STYLE mansion is a reminder of Long Island's Gold Coast of the 1920s. On display are fine European paintings and furnishings. Tours and programs should be of special interest to students studying architecture, art and history. Visitors are advised to make separate arrangements to visit Planting Fields Arboretum, the grounds on which the mansion is located.

Address/Telephone   *Planting Fields Road
Oyster Bay, NY 11771
(516) 922-9210

Website www.plantingfields.org

When to Visit	April 1 to September 30 November to March by appointment Daily—12:15 p.m. to 3:30 p.m. Special-interest groups can be accommodated in the morning by appointment
Charges/Fees	Adults—$5.00; seniors—$3.50; children (7–12)—$1.00
Suggested Grades	6–12
Guided Tour	Programs geared to group interest
Maximum Group	48 (minimum—14)
Group Notice	1 month
Eating Facilities	None
Restroom Facilities	Yes
Handicapped Access	Yes
Additional Information	Appointment necessary. Educational programs available. *Mailing address: Coe Hall, P.O. Box 58, Oyster Bay, NY 11771

Earle-Wightman House
(Oyster Bay Historical Society)

FROM ITS ORIGINAL site on South Street, the Earle-Wightman House witnessed the American Revolution and the exciting role played in it by the Town of Oyster Bay. Built c. 1720, this historic landmark is furnished with period furniture. There is a reference library, changing historical exhibits, and a hands-on program on the Revolutionary War. Also included is a one-room house exhibit that is a replica of early homes on Long Island.

Address/Telephone	*20 Summit Street Oyster Bay, NY 11771 (516) 922-5032 Fax: (516) 922-6892
Website	www.oysterbayhistory.org

When to Visit	Tuesday to Friday—10:00 a.m. to 2:00 p.m. Saturday—9:00 a.m. to 1:00 p.m. Sunday—1:00 p.m. to 4:00 p.m.
Charges/Fees	Donation School groups—$3.00 per student
Suggested Grades	K–Adult
Guided Tour	Yes, hands-on program on Colonial life and Revolutionary War presented to schools and groups
Maximum Group	30, with adequate supervision
Group Notice	2 weeks
Eating Facilities	None
Restroom Facilities	Yes
Handicapped Access	Yes
Additional Information	*Mailing address: P.O. Box 297, Oyster Bay, NY 11771

Oyster Bay National Wildlife Refuge

THIS 3,209-ACRE refuge is one of nine on Long Island, and one of over 500 refuges throughout the United States. Subtidal habitats, salt marshes and a freshwater pond make waterfowl-viewing a treat. Best time to view is winter! Enjoy fishing, wildlife observation, photography and environmental education. Access to the refuge is by boat from Long Island Sound or local boat ramps.

Address/Telephone	*Oyster Bay, NY (631) 286-0485
When to Visit	Daily
Charges/Fees	None
Suggested Grades	K–Adult
Guided Tour	Planned trips by Refuge staff on occasional basis

Maximum Group	20
Group Notice	2 weeks
Eating Facilities	None
Restroom Facilities	Yes, furnished by Town of Oyster Bay
Handicapped Access	Restrooms, parking (Town of Oyster Bay facilities)
Additional Information	Parking is limited to local boat ramps and marinas. Canoe and kayak rentals are available nearby. The Waterfront Center at Oyster Bay offers educational programs for all ages. *Mailing address: P.O. Box 21, Shirley, NY 11967

Planting Fields Arboretum State Historic Park

THIS ARBORETUM WAS formerly the estate of William Robertson Coe. The house was replaced in 1921 after a fire, and is generally considered to be one of the finest examples of Elizabethan/Tudor architecture in America. About 160 acres are developed as an arboretum, which is comprised of thousands of ornamental trees and shrubs from around the world; 40 more acres are lawns, and the remaining 200 are preserved in their natural state. There are two large greenhouse ranges, one devoted to camellias—winter flowering December through March. The Main Greenhouse complex features economic plants of interest (bananas, citrus varieties, coffee, etc.) and collections of orchids, ferns, cacti and succulents, begonias, bromeliads, etc.

Address/Telephone	Planting Fields Road Oyster Bay, NY 11771 (516) 922-8600
Website	www.plantingfields.org
When to Visit	Monday to Sunday 9:00 a.m. to 5:00 p.m. Greenhouses close at 4:30 p.m.

Charges/Fees $5.00 parking fee daily from May 1 to Labor Day and on all holidays and weekends throughout the year.
Schools call for group rates. Senior citizens free Monday to Friday with State pass.

Suggested Grades K–Adult

Guided Tour Call for appointment

Maximum Group Unlimited

Group Notice 1 month

Eating Facilities None

Restroom Facilities Yes

Handicapped Access Yes

Raynham Hall

D ATING FROM 1740, this home of Samuel Townsend, whose son Robert was George Washington's chief spy in New York City, serves the town through a variety of programs. Included are a school program, summer programs and a lecture series for adults. On display are furnishings of the Colonial period plus a beautiful Christmas exhibit each December in the Victorian addition to the house.

Address/Telephone 20 West Main Street
Oyster Bay, NY 11771
(516) 922-6808

Website www.raynhamhallmuseum.org

When to Visit June 1 to Labor Day
Noon to 5:00 p.m.
Tuesday to Sunday
1:00 p.m. to 5:00 p.m. (self-tour)
Morning hours for prearranged tours only

Charges/Fees Adults—$3.00; children under 6—free
Seniors and students over 6—$2.00

Suggested Grades K–Adult

Guided Tour Yes, by reservation only

Maximum Group 30, with one adult per group of 10

Group Notice Call well in advance (for guided tour only)

Eating Facilities Outdoor picnicking (in season)

Restroom Facilities Yes

Handicapped Access Only lower floor accessible

Additional Information Craft and holiday workshops for children and adults by arrangement.
Call for information on summer workshops.
Multimedia available.

Sagamore Hill National Historic Site

SAGAMORE HILL WAS Theodore Roosevelt's permanent home and "summer White House" during his presidency. It contains the historic furnishings and souvenirs from Roosevelt's world travels. The most famous of this Queen Anne–style structure's 23 rooms is the North Room, which truly reflects the spirit of T. R. with its many hunting trophies, books, paintings, flags and furniture. Old Orchard, the former home of General Theodore Roosevelt, Jr., is a museum on the site.

Address/Telephone 20 Sagamore Hill Road
Oyster Bay, NY 11771
(516) 922-4447 (General information)
or (516) 922-4788

Website www.nps.gov/sahi

When to Visit Monday to Sunday
9:00 a.m. to 4:30 p.m.
Closed Monday–Tuesday in the winter

Charges/Fees $5.00 per person—ages 17 and above

Suggested Grades 4–Adult

Guided Tour	Entry to the house is by guided tour only. Tours are every half hour from 9:30 a.m. to 4:00 p.m. Tours are limited to 14 people.
Maximum Group	60, with one adult per group of 8. Group tours are generally scheduled in the morning around 10:00 a.m.
Group Notice	2 weeks to 5 months in advance
Eating Facilities	None. Picnic area available.
Restroom Facilities	Yes (Visitor center and Old Orchard Museum)
Handicapped Access	Restrooms and first floor accessible to wheelchairs.
Additional Information	Films on Theodore Roosevelt at Old Orchard Museum—10 and 20 minutes.

Theodore Roosevelt Sanctuary and Audubon Center

THE OLDEST NATIONAL Audubon Sanctuary in America, this sanctuary occupies 12 acres and is unique in that most of the trees, shrubs and vines were planted specifically to attract birds. The visitors' center displays information about the birds and plants, plus exhibits on Theodore Roosevelt and the Conservation Movement. The sanctuary offers workshops and public programs for children and adults, conducts avian research and specializes in natural science and environmental education programs.

Address/Telephone	134 Cove Road Oyster Bay, NY 11771 (516) 922-3200 Fax: (516) 922-6734 Email: trsanct@aol.com
When to Visit	Monday to Friday—8:00 a.m. to 4:30 p.m. Saturday and Sunday—1:00 p.m. to 4:30 p.m. Grounds: Monday to Friday—8:00 a.m. to 4:30 p.m. Saturday and Sunday—9:00 a.m. to 4:30 p.m.
Charges/Fees	Donation Program—call for information
Suggested Grades	Pre-K–Adult

Theodore Roosevelt and family at Sagamore Hill

Guided Tour	Self-guided tour. Programs and tours arranged for groups at a fee.
Maximum Group	50
Group Notice	2 weeks
Eating Facilities	None
Restroom Facilities	Yes
Handicapped Access	Yes
Additional Information	Education brochures and materials on request.

The Townsend Genealogical Society and Museum

THIS LOVELY VICTORIAN house contains furnishings and documents which tell the stories of the members of the Townsend family. The members of this family were descendants of John, Richard and Henry Townsend, who were among the earliest settlers of Oyster Bay.

Address/Telephone	107 E. Main Street
	Oyster Bay, NY 11771
	(516) 922-5434
	Email: townsend-society@worldnet.att.net
Website	www.townsendsociety.org
When to Visit	By appointment
Charges/Fees	$1.00 donation suggested
Suggested Grades	Adults preferred
Guided Tour	Yes, 30 minutes or longer
Maximum Group	10 adults
Group Notice	1 week
Eating Facilities	None
Restroom Facilities	Yes
Handicapped Access	No

WLIW 21

WLIW 21 IS a public television station serving the residents of the tri-state area. Channel 21 is located in Plainview, along the border of Nassau and Suffolk Counties. Visitors will be given a tour of the production studio, master control, editing suites and tape library.

Address/Telephone	*Channel 21 Drive
	Plainview, NY 11803
	(516) 367-2100
Website	www.wliw.org

When to Visit	Write or call for appointment
Charges/Fees	None
Suggested Grades	7–Adult
Guided Tour	Yes, 30 minutes
Maximum Group	10
Group Notice	14 days
Eating Facilities	None
Restroom Facilities	Yes
Handicapped Access	Yes
Additional Information	*Mailing address: Public Information Dept., 303 Sunnyside Blvd., P.O. Box 21, Plainview, NY 11803, Attn: Tour Director

The Dodge House
(Cow Neck Peninsula Historical Society)

THE DODGE HOUSE, a National and State designated Landmark, is maintained and managed by the Cow Neck Peninsula Historical Society. Built c. 1721 by Thomas Dodge and home to succeeding generations of Dodges until 1991, the brown cedar shingled building is a rare surviving example of an early 18th-century farmhouse on its original site. Now a museum, it is filled with a centuries-old collection of Dodge family treasures and trivia—furniture, documents, china, wrought ironware, memorabilia, etc. A handcrafted tool collection is of special interest to many.

Address/Telephone	58 Harbor Road Port Washington, NY 11050 (516) 767-3970
Website	www.cowneck.org
When to Visit	By appointment only
Charges/Fees	Adults—$2.50; children—$1.00
Suggested Grades	4–Adult
Guided Tour	Yes

Maximum Group	Call for information
Group Notice	2 weeks
Eating Facilities	None
Restroom Facilities	Yes
Handicapped Access	Yes

Polish-American Museum

THE POLISH-AMERICAN Museum features exhibits on Poles and Polish-Americans who have made valuable contributions to medicine, education, science, arts and political thought. Many paintings, drawings and pictures of Polish heros such as Generals Casimir Pulaski and Thaddeus Kosciuszko adorn the museum. A bilingual research library as well as historical documents and cultural artifacts are available for the use or observation of interested visitors.

Address/Telephone	16 Bellview Avenue
	Port Washington, NY 11050
	(516) 883-6542
	Fax: (516) 767-1936
When to Visit	Tuesday to Friday—10:00 a.m. to 2:00 p.m.
	Saturday and Sunday—By appointment
Charges/Fees	Donation
Suggested Grades	4–Adult
Guided Tour	Yes, 60 to 90 minutes
Maximum Group	20
Group Notice	1 week
Eating Facilities	None
Restroom Facilities	Yes
Handicapped Access	No

Port Washington Water Pollution Control District

VISITORS WILL OBSERVE the operation of a water pollution control plant utilizing primary and secondary sewage treatment with sludge incineration. The final process of incineration permits total sterilization of sludge by-products, reduces volume and prevents the need to dump effluents in our coastal waters.

Address/Telephone	*70 Harbor Road Port Washington, NY 11050 (516) 944-6100
When to Visit	Fair-weather months only 10:00 a.m. to 3:00 p.m. By appointment
Charges/Fees	None
Suggested Grades	6–Adult
Guided Tour	Yes, 30 to 45 minutes
Maximum Group	20, with 1 adult
Group Notice	2 weeks
Eating Facilities	None
Restroom Facilities	None
Handicapped Access	No
Additional Information	*Mailing address: P.O. Box 790, Port Washington, NY 11050

Sands Point Preserve

THIS 216-ACRE PRESERVE is a former Gold Coast estate located on Long Island Sound. Once owned by the Gould and the Guggenheim families, these magnificent, castle-like buildings now house changing exhibits. "Falaise," the beautiful Normandy-style manor house owned by Harry

Guggenheim and Alicia Patterson, which still holds all the family art and furnishings, is open for guided tours. Castlegould features changeable exhibits with natural history themes. Hempstead House has an extensive exhibit of items from the Buten Wedgwood Ceramics collection.

Address/Telephone	Sands Point Preserve
	95 Middle Neck Road
	Port Washington, NY 11050
	Falaise and Preserve: (516) 571-7900
Website	www.co.nassau.ny.us/parks
When to Visit	Preserve and special exhibits: Tuesday to Sunday
	Falaise: Wednesday to Sunday
	May to October—Noon to 3:00 p.m.
	Wedgwood: Saturday and Sunday
	May to October—12:30 p.m. to 4:30 p.m.
Charges/Fees	Falaise tour: Ages 10 and up—$5.00; seniors—$4.00
	Call for group rates and arrangement
	Wedgwood collection—$2.00
Suggested Grades	7–Adult
Guided Tour	Yes, 1 hour (Falaise)
Maximum Group	45
Group Notice	3 weeks
Eating Facilities	Picnic facilities (no grills)
Restroom Facilities	Yes
Handicapped Access	Yes—special exhibits
	No—Falaise and Wedgwood collection
Additional Information	Gift Shop. Operated by the Nassau County Department of Recreation and Parks.

Sands-Willets House
(Cow Neck Peninsula Historical Society)

THE SANDS-WILLETS HOUSE, a National and State designated Landmark, presently serves as the Cow Neck Peninsula Historical Society's Museum. Featured are rooms and furnishings of the Colonial, Empire and Victorian periods. The original building which dates back to 1735 has a restored outer kitchen with a beehive oven and an open hearth fireplace for cooking and baking. A 1690 Dutch barn located on the property exhibits antique tools, carriages and local memorabilia. Exhibits will be changed.

Address/Telephone	336 Port Washington Boulevard
	Port Washington, NY 11050
	(516) 365-9074
Website	www.cowneck.org
When to Visit	Sunday—2:00 p.m. to 4:30 p.m. and by appointment
Charges/Fees	Adults—$2.50; children—$1.00
Suggested Grades	K–Adult
Guided Tour	Yes. Call for information regarding group tours, lectures, and craft and cooking programs.
Maximum Group	30
Group Notice	1 month
Eating Facilities	None
Restroom Facilities	Yes
Handicapped Access	No
Additional Information	Caution around antiques

The Phillips House Museum

THE PHILLIPS HOUSE is one of the Victorian homes surviving from an era when influential, well-to-do sea captains lived in Rockville Centre. Built around 1882, the house blends the decorative style of the Victorian period with the classical simplicity found in New England cottages.

Address/Telephone	28 Hempstead Avenue
	Rockville Centre, NY 11570
	(516) 678-9201

When to Visit	Saturday and Sunday
	1:00 p.m. to 4:00 p.m.
	Weekdays by appointment
	Closed Saturday in July and August
Charges/Fees	None
Suggested Grades	K–Adult
Guided Tour	Yes, by appointment
Maximum Group	35
Group Notice	2 weeks
Eating Facilities	Picnic facilities
Restroom Facilities	Yes
Handicapped Access	No

Bryant Library Local History Collection

VISITORS MAY OBSERVE and use this specialized research collection, which includes the works of literary greats such as William Cullen Bryant and Christopher Morley. Also, many primary documents and works of local historians serve as part of the library's collection. First established in 1878, the library is the oldest continuing one on Long Island.

Address/Telephone	2 Paper Mill Road
	Roslyn, NY 11576
	(516) 621-2240
When to Visit	Monday—9:00 a.m. to 2:00 p.m.
	Tuesday—10:30 a.m. to 7:00 p.m.
	Wednesday—10:00 a.m. to 5:00 p.m.
	Thursday and Friday—9:00 a.m. to 5:00 p.m.
	One Saturday of each month—9:00 a.m. to 5:00 p.m.
	Hours may vary. Please call for appointment.
Charges/Fees	None
Suggested Grades	10–Adult
Guided Tour	By arrangement
Maximum Group	20

Group Notice	2 months
Eating Facilities	None
Restroom Facilities	Yes
Handicapped Access	Yes

Nassau County Museum of Art

THE MUSEUM OCCUPIES the elegant neo-Georgian mansion of the Frick country estate, situated on 145 beautifully landscaped acres in the heart of Long Island's historic North Shore. Featuring ten refurbished galleries, the Museum produces four major art exhibitions per year. In addition, there are formal gardens, a unique trellis, ponds and a wild-flower walk that provides a sequence of delightful vistas in which to enjoy nature and one of the largest sculpture gardens on the east coast.

Address/Telephone	*One Museum Drive
	(Off Northern Boulevard)
	Roslyn, NY 11576
	(516) 484-9337 (Call for events information)
Website	www.nassaumuseum.com
When to Visit	Tuesday to Sunday
	11:00 a.m. to 5:00 p.m.
Charges/Fees	Adults—$6.00; seniors—$5.00; children
	and students—$4.00
Suggested Grades	K–Adult
Guided Tour	Free with admission every Tuesday through
	Saturday at 2:00 p.m. or by appointment
	for groups
Maximum Group	50—by appointment
Group Notice	3 to 4 weeks
Eating Facilities	Museum café located in museum, serving light
	lunch from noon to 3:00 p.m., Tuesday to
	Sunday.
Restroom Facilities	Yes

Handicapped Access Yes, special ramps and signage for handicapped persons; restroom

Additional Information Museum Gift Shop offers many unusual and attractive items, including Museum replicas, jewelry and art-related stationery. Museum Bookstore/Gallery offers a wide selection of art publications, posters and scholarly books for art students. Call Alison (516) 484-9338 x11 to ask about art classes for adults and children.
*Mailing address: One Museum Dr., Roslyn Harbor, NY 11576

Tee Ridder Miniatures Museum
(of the Nassau County Museum of Art)

THE TEE RIDDER Miniatures Museum of the Nassau County Museum of Art houses 26 miniature rooms recessed in the walls, ranging from cozy kitchens to elegant gilded drawing rooms; a dollhouse designed after Carter's Grove in Williamsburg; and 5 showcases containing fine furniture, ceramics, silver, and paintings created by famous artisans. There are also another 20 rooms that are available for viewing. These creations of Madeleine "Tee" Ridder will delight visitors of all ages. The museum also features changing exhibitions, varying from creations by local schools to the Kupjack rooms from the Winterthur Museum.

Address/Telephone 15 Museum Drive
Roslyn Harbor, NY 11576
(516) 484-7841

Website www.nassaumuseum.com

When to Visit Tuesday to Sunday
11:00 a.m. to 5:00 p.m.

Charges/Fees Adults—$6.00; seniors—$5.00; students and children—$4.00 (includes admission to the Nassau County Museum of Art)

Suggested Grades All ages

Guided Tour Scavenger hunt for children
Groups by appointment

Maximum Group 50

Group Notice 2 weeks

Eating Facilities None

Restroom Facilities Yes

Handicapped Access Yes

Additional Information Charming gift shop with items for the miniature enthusiast, such as how-to books, furniture, accessories and much more. There are also many gift items and books for the non-miniaturist.

Sea Cliff Village Museum
(Village of Sea Cliff)

HOUSED IN A former Methodist parsonage, the museum focuses on the history of Sea Cliff with particular emphasis on the period between the early 1880s through the 1940s. Changing exhibits, a permanent display of early Sea Cliff photographs and a Victorian kitchen are included.

Address/Telephone 95 Tenth Avenue
Sea Cliff, NY 11579
(516) 671-0090 or (516) 671-0080

When to Visit Weekends
September to June
2:00 p.m. to 5:00 p.m.
Weekday groups by appointment

Charges/Fees $1.00 per person

Suggested Grades K–Adult

Guided Tour Yes, with slide program, 1 hour

Maximum Group 25

Group Notice	2 weeks
Eating Facilities	None
Restroom Facilities	Yes
Handicapped Access	First floor only

Seaford Historical Society and Museum

THE SEAFORD HISTORICAL Society and Museum, housed in a building built in 1893, once served as a two-room schoolhouse for the Seaford community and from 1919 to 1975 as a firehouse and community hall. The museum now contains many artifacts and memorabilia that reflect the farming and fishing life along the South Shore in the early days of the century, including tools, clothing, books, furniture and photos. Of special interest is a "Seaford skiff" built in 1906 and used by baymen to hunt and fish in the Great South Bay. The museum has been designated as a landmark by the Town of Hempstead.

Address/Telephone	*3890 Waverly Avenue Seaford, NY 11783 (516) 826-1150
When to Visit	By appointment
Charges/Fees	Donation
Suggested Grades	4–Adult
Guided Tour	Yes, 30 to 60 minutes
Maximum Group	35
Group Notice	1 week
Eating Facilities	None
Restroom Facilities	Yes
Handicapped Access	No
Additional Information	*Mailing address: Seaford Historical Society and Museum, 2234 Jackson Ave., Seaford, NY 11783

Tackapausha Museum and Preserve

A REGIONAL MUSEUM of natural history, often referred to as the Life Sciences facility, it features exhibits depicting Long Island plant and animal life. An 80-acre preserve and 5 miles of nature trails adjoin the museum.

Address/Telephone Washington Avenue
Seaford, NY 11783
(516) 571-7443

When to Visit Museum—Tuesday to Saturday 10:00 a.m.
to 4:00 p.m.
Sunday—1:00 p.m. to 4:00 p.m.
Preserve—8:00 a.m. to sunset

Charges/Fees Adults—$2.00; children 5 and over—$1.00

Suggested Grades K–Adult

Guided Tour Yes, 1 hour

Maximum Group 30

Group Notice Call for appointment

Eating Facilities Picnic facilities

Restroom Facilities Yes

Handicapped Access Yes

Additional Information Wear appropriate clothing and footwear for walking in preserve; tour given rain or shine. Collection of natural material is prohibited. Operated by the Nassau County Department of Recreation and Parks.

Town of Oyster Bay Animal Shelter

A T THIS PUBLIC shelter, visitors will learn how stray animals are picked up, how care is provided for them and how they, as well as abandoned animals, are relocated to new homes.

Address/Telephone 150 Miller Place
Syosset, NY 11791
(516) 677-5784

When to Visit	Monday to Friday 10:00 a.m. to 2:00 p.m.
Charges/Fees	None
Suggested Grades	1 and up
Guided Tour	Yes, 15 to 25 minutes
Maximum Group	25
Group Notice	1 week
Eating Facilities	None
Restroom Facilities	Emergency only
Handicapped Access	Yes

Nassau Veterans Memorial Coliseum

HOME OF THE NHL New York Islanders and the AFL New York Dragons, the Nassau Veterans Memorial Coliseum features sporting events, trade shows, concerts, family shows and other forms of entertainment.

Address/Telephone	Nassau Veterans Memorial Coliseum 1255 Hempstead Turnpike Uniondale, NY 11553-1200 (516) 794-9303
Website	www.nassaucoliseum.com
When to Visit	Varies with program
Charges/Fees	Varies with program
Suggested Grades	Pre-K–Adult
Guided Tour	None
Maximum Group	Unlimited (minimum eligible for group fee—20)
Group Notice	1 month or more depending on popularity
Eating Facilities	Yes
Restroom Facilities	Yes
Handicapped Access	Yes
Additional Information	Group sales office open Monday to Friday— 9:00 a.m. to 5:00 p.m. Box office open 9:30 a.m. to 4:45 p.m. (Open later on event days)

Jones Beach State Park

WHAT MAY BE Long Island's most celebrated beach complex is located on the South Shore in Wantagh, approximately 35 miles from New York City. Swimming in eight Atlantic Ocean bathing areas and Zachs Bay. East and West Bathhouses feature Olympic-size pools, diving areas and wading pools. In addition, each bathhouse includes lockers and showers for the convenience of pool and ocean bathers.

Fishermen delight in the many types of fishing available. A bait station and fishing piers can be used for bay fishing at Field 10, while beach areas at West End 2 and Field 6 are designated for surf casting (night fishing by permit). The West End Boat Basin (east of Jones Inlet) offers daytime berths, pump-out station, mooring area, comfort stations and refreshment stand.

Surfboarding is permitted at the West End 2 area from the Monday after Thanksgiving through Labor Day. There is a 2-mile-long boardwalk with deck games, softball fields, fitness course, dancing nightly at bandshell, concerts, special events, miniature golf and basketball.

Address/Telephone	Jones Beach State Park P.O. Box 1000 Wantagh, NY 11793 (516) 785-1600
Website	www.nysparks.com
When to Visit	Daily Sunrise to sunset Sunrise until midnight—3rd weekend in June to Labor Day Swimming from Memorial Day to mid-September

Charges/Fees	$7.00 per car (daily)—Memorial Day to
	   mid-September
	$5.00 per car (weekends)—April to Memorial Day
	   and mid-September to beginning of December

Guided Tour	None
Maximum Group	Write (see below) or call for information
Group Notice	Write (see below) or call for information
Eating Facilities	Picnic areas, boardwalk with concession stands, Jones Beach Restaurant
Restroom Facilities	Yes
Handicapped Access	Yes

Additional Information Applications for group outing permits for all Long Island State Park facilities may be obtained by sending a stamped, self-addressed envelope to: Group Outings, P.O. Box 247, Babylon, NY 11702. Allow 10 days from date of postmark for processing of permit.

Jones Beach Theater

THIS OPEN AMPHITHEATER, seating approximately 14,500 people, was originally the Jones Beach Marine Theater. This theater has undergone a multi-million dollar redesign and reconstruction program and is now a modern state-of-the-art facility. It is the site where musical groups perform in concert. Famous stars such as Frank Sinatra and Billy Joel have played and sung to capacity audiences at the Jones Beach Theater.

Address/Telephone *Jones Beach State Park
Wantagh, NY 11793
(516) 221-1000

Website www.livetonight.com

When to Visit June, July and August
Monday to Saturday—10:00 a.m. to 6:00 p.m.
Sunday—12:00 p.m. to 6:00 p.m.
Shows: June to September
Show times: 7:00 p.m.

Charges/Fees Write or call for season schedule

Suggested Grades Varies with performance

Guided Tour None

Maximum Group Unlimited

Group Notice As much as possible. Call as early as Memorial Day.

Eating Facilities Yes

Restroom Facilities Yes

Handicapped Access Yes

Additional Information *Mailing address: New York State Office of Parks, Recreation and Historic Preservation, Long Island Region, Belmont Lake State Park, P.O. Box 247, Babylon, NY 11702, (631) 669-1000.

Twin Lakes Preserve
(Town of Hempstead)

THE TWIN LAKES PRESERVE, located on Old Mill Road in Wantagh, is dedicated to the understanding, preservation and enjoyment of Long Island's natural environment. The 58-acre preserve features five fresh-water ponds and extensive sections of wet woodlands. In its picturesque and serene setting, residents may partake of such outdoor activities as bird watching, sportfishing or hiking and exploring along a trail system.

Address/Telephone	*Old Mill Road Wantagh, NY 11793 (516) 766-1580
When to Visit	Monday to Sunday—Dawn to dusk
Charges/Fees	None
Suggested Grades	All ages
Guided Tour	None
Eating Facilities	No
Restroom Facilities	No
Handicapped Access	No
Additional Information	*Mailing address: Marine Nature Study Area, 500 Slice Drive, Oceanside, NY 11572

Wantagh Preservation Society Museum

THIS MUSEUM IS housed in an 1885 railroad station and 1912 railroad parlor car. Also on site is Wantagh's c. 1907 rural post office. In their restored states, they afford the visitor the opportunity to glimpse an important part of life at the turn of the century. Also on display are pho-tographs depicting life in turn-of-the-century Wantagh. The museum is listed on the State and National Register of Historic Places.

Address/Telephone	Wantagh Avenue opposite Emeric Avenue P.O. Box 132 Wantagh, NY 11793 (516) 826-8767—Call during museum hours. (516) 826-1150—Leave message
Website	www.wantagh.li

When to Visit April to October
Sunday—2:00 p.m. to 4:00 p.m.
Closed November to March

Charges/Fees Donation

Suggested Grades 4–Adult

Guided Tour Yes, by arrangement

Maximum Group 25

Group Notice 2 weeks

Eating Facilities None

Restroom Facilities Yes

Handicapped Access No

Additional Information Slide show available by arrangement. Special events on museum grounds—call for schedule.

Hempstead Resource Recovery, Inc.
(American Ref-Fuel Company of Hempstead)

VISITORS WILL OBSERVE the latest technology in solid waste resource recovery. This facility, which is New York's largest waste-to-energy plant, converts municipal solid waste into electricity. Enough electricity is produced at this plant to supply the electrical energy needs for 65,000 suburban homes. Metals are recovered from the ash by-product and marketed.

Address/Telephone 600 Merchants Concourse
Westbury, NY 11590
(516) 683-5400

When to Visit By appointment

Charges/Fees None

Suggested Grades 5–Adult

Guided Tour Yes, 1 hour

Maximum Group 30, with one adult per group of 10

Group Notice 1 month

Eating Facilities None

Restroom Facilities Yes
Handicapped Access No
Additional Information Published information furnished upon request.

Hicks Nurseries, Inc.

THIS FAMILY-ORIENTED landmark Long Island business, now in its sixth generation of family ownership, does more than just sell the traditional plants, tools and nursery supplies. During the holiday seasons, displays are set up depicting a theme or story. These free, animated shows bring original garden and nature-oriented tales to life as visitors walk among the various scenes. Halloween offers an adventure of Otto the Ghost, apples and pumpkins for sale and wagon rides. Christmas tells a holiday story and offers visits with Santa Claus. During both seasons there is a live farm animal zoo. Springtime, the most colorful of all seasons, brings bunnies and flowers, and presents the Annual Flower and Garden Show, with display gardens, lectures and demonstrations. Workshops and lectures on a wide range of horticultural topics such as herbs, houseplants, lawns, trees and gardens are scheduled throughout the year. There is no admission or parking charge for any events, but there are fees for some workshops.

Address/Telephone 100 Jericho Turnpike
Westbury, NY 11590
(516) 334-0066

When to Visit Halloween Season—late-September to October 31
Christmas Season—mid-November to December 26
Spring Flower and Garden Show—mid-March

Charges/Fees None

Suggested Grades All ages

Guided Tour None

Maximum Group Varies, call for information

Group Notice Varies, call for information

Eating Facilities None

Restroom Facilities Yes

Handicapped Access Yes

Additional Information There is a free quarterly newsletter that provides details and dates for all events and provides useful gardening information. Call to be put on the mailing list. Free membership in the Hicks Nurseries Gardeners Advantage Program brings information on special member sales and programs.

Westbury Music Fair

OFFERING THE ONLY example of a professional theater-in-the-round in the metropolitan area, Westbury Music Fair features a variety of plays, musicals and concerts. Scheduled throughout the year during holidays and summertime are full-scale productions designed to appeal to children such as *Peter Rabbit, Raggedy Ann and Andy, Hansel and Gretel* and *Goldilocks and the Three Bears*.

Address/Telephone 960 Brush Hollow Road
Westbury, NY 11590
(516) 334-0800—Automated information line
(516) 333-2101—Group Sales Office

Website www.musicfair.com

When to Visit Write or call for schedule

Charges/Fees Varies with program

Suggested Grades All ages—depending on program

Guided Tour None

Maximum Group 2,742

Group Notice Early as possible, depending on popularity of program

Eating Facilities Yes

Restroom Facilities Yes

Handicapped Access Yes

SUFFOLK COUNTY

The Amelia Cottage Museum
(Amagansett Historical Association)

B UILT IN 1725 and moved to its present site in 1794, the museum displays furnishings from many periods of history, but especially a fine collection of Dominy furniture. Featuring a unique divided staircase, the cottage also boasts much of the original knife-and-groove paneling as well as iron, hand-wrought hinges and outer hardware, and a huge fireplace.

Address/Telephone Montauk Highway and Windmill Lane
Amagansett, NY 11930
(631) 267-3020

When to Visit Friday to Sunday
10:00 a.m. to 4:00 p.m.

Charges/Fees Adults—$2.00; children—$1.00

Suggested Grades K–Adult

Guided Tour None, curator on duty

Maximum Group 30, with one adult per group of 15

Group Notice 10 days

Eating Facilities None

Restroom Facilities Yes

Handicapped Access No

East Hampton Town Marine Museum
(East Hampton Historical Society)

L OCATED ON 36 acres overlooking the sea, this museum displays, in interpretive exhibits, artifacts and descriptions of the traditions and working life of local fishermen. Through them one traces the development of the fishing and whaling industries of the past three centuries and learns the lore and technology of boating for work and for leisure.

Address/Telephone	*Atlantic Avenue and Bluff Road Amagansett, NY 11930 (631) 267-6544
When to Visit	Saturday and Sunday—June and September Daily—July 4 to Labor Day 10:00 a.m. to 5:00 p.m. Winter: By appointment Groups call for appointment during season and winter months
Charges/Fees	Adults—$4.00; children and seniors—$2.00 Please call for discounted group rates
Suggested Grades	K–Adult
Guided Tour	By appointment
Maximum Group	40, with adequate supervision
Group Notice	2 weeks
Eating Facilities	Picnic facilities
Restroom Facilities	Yes
Handicapped Access	Limited
Additional Information	*Mailing address: 101 Main Street, East Hampton, NY 11937 (631) 324-6850

The Roy K. Lester Carriage Museum
(Amagansett Historical Association)

A COLLECTION OF 27 carriages displayed in two large barns, ranging from delicate buggies and elegant formal carriages to a full-size replica of a Heavy Concord Stagecoach. These vehicles are a wonderful marriage of art and engineering, utility and elegance. The collection brings back to life a form of transportation that was predominant for many years. Some of the carriages have been fully restored, but most are in original condition.

Address/Telephone	Montauk Highway and Windmill Lane
	Amagansett, NY 11930
	(631) 267-3020
When to Visit	Friday to Sunday
	10:00 a.m. to 4:00 p.m.
Charges/Fees	Adults—$2.00; children—$1.00
Suggested Grades	K–Adult
Guided Tour	None, curator on duty
Maximum Group	30, with one adult per group of 15
Group Notice	10 days
Eating Facilities	None
Restroom Facilities	Yes
Handicapped Access	Yes

Lauder Museum
(Amityville Historical Society)

THIS MUSEUM, ONCE the Bank of Amityville, serves as the attractive home for memorabilia of Amityville's past. Here this material is collected, preserved and exhibited. It is also from this point that a self-guided historical walking tour of Amityville begins.

Address/Telephone	170 Broadway and Ireland Place
	Amityville, NY 11701
	(631) 598-1486
	Fax: (631) 598-7399
When to Visit	Tuesday, Friday and Sunday
	2:00 p.m. to 4:00 p.m.
	Groups by appointment
Charges/Fees	Donations accepted
Suggested Grades	1–9
Guided Tour	Yes, 1 hour by arrangement
Maximum Group	30, with one adult per group of 10
Group Notice	2 weeks
Eating Facilities	None
Restroom Facilities	Yes
Handicapped Access	Ramp for handicapped

Eaton's Neck Coast Guard Station and Lighthouse

THIS COAST GUARD station serves as a base for search and rescue operations. A communications center, weather observation post, boats and lighthouse are part of the facility. The tour includes the main building and a close-up view of the boats. Visitors will have a chance to meet the personnel, view the facilities and see a 200-year-old lighthouse. Other areas of the station's responsibility include Law Enforcement and Marine Pollution Investigation.

Address/Telephone	*Ocean Avenue to Eaton's Neck to Lighthouse Road
	Asharoken, NY 11768
	(631) 261-6959 Call: Operations Officer
When to Visit	Not open to the general public; groups only, by appointment
	9:00 a.m. to 11:00 a.m. and 1:00 p.m. to 4:00 p.m.

Charges/Fees	None
Suggested Grades	2–Adult
Guided Tour	Yes, 45 minutes
Maximum Group	30, with adequate supervision
Group Notice	1 month
Eating Facilities	None
Restroom Facilities	Emergency only
Handicapped Access	No
Additional Information	*Mailing address: Northport, NY 11768

Great South Bay Cruises and Excursions (Moonchaser)

T HE MOONCHASER OFFERS groups and the general public the opportunity to enjoy the picturesque scenery surrounding Great South Bay. Fully equipped with an enclosed maindeck and canopied upper sun deck, this vessel offers comfort and enjoyment whether used for a general excursion or catered affair. A variety of cruises and experiences are offered or may be specially arranged.

Address/Telephone	*Captree State Park Captree Boat Basin Babylon, NY 11702 (631) 661-5061
When to Visit	Daily May to October Call for arrangements
Charges/Fees	Call for information
Suggested Grades	Pre-K–Adult
Guided Tour	90-minute narrative sightseeing tour July 4 to Labor Day
Maximum Group	250 per boat

Group Notice	Advance notice advised
Eating Facilities	Beverages available—"brown bag"
Restroom Facilities	Yes
Handicapped Access	Limited
Additional Information	Dinner cruises to Fire Island. Excursions from July 4 to Labor Day. *Mailing address: P.O. Box 274, West Islip, NY 11795

Village of Babylon Historical and Preservation Society

HOUSED IN A building that was formerly the Babylon Village Library, this museum contains artifacts, photographs and memorabilia relative to Babylon and West Islip history. There is an old horsedrawn carriage, textiles, quilts, clothing, antique farming tools, a blacksmith's bellows and a grassboat with decoys. Also displayed are old toys and home items such as a butter churn and sewing machine. In addition, there are exhibits that change periodically.

Address/Telephone	*117 W. Main Street Babylon, NY 11702 (631) 669-7086
When to Visit	Wednesday and Saturday 2:00 p.m. to 4:00 p.m. Groups by appointment
Charges/Fees	Donation
Suggested Grades	3–Adult
Guided Tour	None
Maximum Group	25, with adequate supervision
Group Notice	1 week
Eating Facilities	None
Restroom Facilities	Yes

Handicapped Access Yes

Additional Information School-term history tour of Babylon Village available for school groups. Call for arrangements.
*Mailing address: P.O. Box 484, Babylon, NY 11702

Bayport Aerodrome Society Museum

THE BAYPORT AERODROME Society is a membership organization formed
in 1972 for the primary purpose of preserving the style and tradition
of aviation in the early 20th century (together with the turf airfield at Bayport, New York). Since its formation, the Society has built 24 hangars housing antique and classic aircraft from Aeroncas to Wacos. The Society has
also created a Museum Hangar for aircraft display and exhibitions. This
hangar is fully heated and also houses the meeting area and library.

Address/Telephone *Vitamin Drive (formerly Cartwright Loop)
off Church Street
Bayport, NY 11705
(631) 472-2405—Leave message
(631) 472-8997
(516) 741-3637 (Pres.)

Website www.bayportaerodrome.org

When to Visit All visits by appointment only
1st and 3rd Sunday of the month
11:00 a.m. to 4:00 p.m.
Other times by special arrangement

Charges/Fees None

Suggested Grades K–Adult

Guided Tour Yes, 30 minutes

Maximum Group 15

Group Notice 1 week

Eating Facilities None

Restroom Facilities Yes

Handicapped Access No

Additional Information *Mailing address: P.O. Box 728, Bayport, NY 11705

Bay Shore Historical Society
(Gibson-Mack-Holt House, c. 1820)

THE GIBSON-MACK-HOLT HOUSE (c. 1820), headquarters of the Bay Shore Historical Society, is one of Bay Shore's oldest homes. It has been restored and furnished to the 1850s, when it was a local tradesman's residence. Features include a tin-lined pantry, cast-iron stove, two-seater outhouse, original chicken coop, Victorian herb garden and flower garden, as well as changing displays of Bay Shore memorabilia.

Address/Telephone	22 Maple Avenue Bay Shore, NY 11706 (631) 665-4637
When to Visit	Tuesday and Saturday—2:00 p.m. to 4:00 p.m. Closed January and February Groups by appointment
Charges/Fees	None
Suggested Grades	4–Adult
Guided Tour	Yes
Maximum Group	30
Group Notice	3 weeks
Eating Facilities	None
Restroom Facilities	Emergency only
Handicapped Access	Yes
Additional Information	Gift shop on premises.

Southside Hospital

THIS VOLUNTARY, NONPROFIT community hospital offers tours of the Radiology Department, Laboratory, Computer Center and other facilities. The day-to-day operations of a modern hospital will be observed by visitors.

Address/Telephone	301 East Main Street Bay Shore, NY 11706 (631) 968-3477

When to Visit	Monday to Friday 9:00 a.m. to 5:00 p.m. Other hours by appointment
Charges/Fees	None
Suggested Grades	8–Adult
Guided Tour	Yes, 1 hour
Maximum Group	15, with 2 adults
Group Notice	3 weeks
Eating Facilities	Yes
Restroom Facilities	Yes
Handicapped Access	Yes
Additional Information	Call for special dates and accommodations for larger groups.

Bellport-Brookhaven Historical Society Barn Museum Complex

A VISIT TO THE museum complex offers exhibits on sea captains, ship building, whaling, market gunning, decoys, Elmer Sperry inventions and everyday life in the 17th, 18th and 19th centuries. On the grounds is a fully equipped blacksmith shop, milk house and 1833 Post-Crowell House. The Exchange Shop features small antiques, prints, paintings, silver and furniture and accepts consignments on Thursday from 10:00 a.m. to 12:00 p.m. The Brown building houses a collection of Early American Decoration, dolls and paperweights. The meeting room is available for use by local groups.

Address/Telephone	12 Bell Street and 31 Bellport Lane Bellport, NY 11713 (631) 286-0888
When to Visit	Thursday to Saturday Memorial Day to Labor Day 1:00 p.m. to 4:30 p.m.
Charges/Fees	None
Suggested Grades	1–Adult
Guided Tour	Yes, by appointment

Maximum Group 30, with adequate supervision

Group Notice 1 week

Eating Facilities Yes, nearby

Restroom Facilities Yes

Handicapped Access Rampway

Additional Information Exchange shop open Thursday to Saturday—11:00 a.m. to 5:00 p.m., Memorial Day to December 20. Consignments accepted Wednesdays from 10:00 a.m. to 12:00 p.m.

Airport Playhouse

THE AIRPORT PLAYHOUSE in Bohemia is a year-round, nonprofit theater now entering its twenty-fifth year. In addition to its annual roster of ten full-scale productions, it also offers a year-round selection of Children's Theater, acting classes, birthday parties, educational theater and much more. For further information please call (631) 589-7588.

Address/Telephone 218 Knickerbocker Avenue
P.O. Box 162
Bohemia, NY 11716
(631) 589-7588

Website www.airportplayhouse.com

When to Visit Box Office Hours:
Tuesday to Saturday—10:00 a.m. to 4:00 p.m. and during showtimes
Call for specific shows/schedules.

Charges/Fees Main Stage Productions—$16.00–$18.00
Children's Theater—$7.00
Call for pricing on Special events/
Performances/Group rates/Senior Specials
Special Events

Suggested Grades Pre-K–Adult, depending on production

Guided Tour Not available at time of print

Maximum Group 279

Group Notice Approximately 2 weeks
Eating Facilities Concession on premises
Restroom Facilities Yes
Handicapped Access Call for arrangements

The Bridge Hampton Historical Society Museum & Archive Complex

THE CORWITH HOUSE Museum, c. 1840, with 1870s additions, offers furnished period rooms, special exhibitions, local history library, document and photo archives, and costume and toy collections. The Strong Wheelwright Shop is an 1870s working blacksmith shop displaying carriages, wagons and farm implements. The Hildreth-Simons Machine Shop and Tractor Barns display antique steam and gasoline engines, tractors and farm machinery. Also on site is the 1907 Bridgehampton Jail.

Address/Telephone *Main Street at Corwith Avenue
Bridgehampton, NY 11932
(631) 537-1088
Fax: (631) 537-4225
Email: bhhs@hamptons.com

Website www.hamptons.com/bhhs

When to Visit March 1 to May 30
Monday to Friday—11:00 a.m. to 4:00 p.m.
June 1 to September 15
Tuesday to Saturday—11:00 a.m. to 4:00 p.m.
September 16 to December 31
Monday to Friday—11:00 a.m. to 4:00 p.m.
Closed January and February
Open year-round by appointment

Charges/Fees $1.00 for adults or donation;
children under 12—free

Suggested Grades 3–Adult

Guided Tour Yes, 30 minutes to 1 hour

Maximum Group	50
Group Notice	2 weeks
Eating Facilities	"Brown bag"
Restroom Facilities	No
Handicapped Access	Yes, limited
Additional Information	*Mailing address: P.O. Box 977, Bridgehampton, NY 11932

DIA Center for the Arts
(The Dan Flavin Institute)

T HE INSTITUTE IS located in the renovated local Hook and Ladder Co. No. 1 (1908) and First Baptist Church Building (1924). It contains a permanent exhibition of the fluorescent-light sculpture of Dan Flavin.

Address/Telephone	*Corwith Avenue
	Bridgehampton, NY 11932
	(631) 537-1476
	Email: info@diacenter.org
Website	www.diacenter.org
When to Visit	Thursday to Sunday
	Memorial Day to September
	Noon to 6:00 p.m.
Charges/Fees	None
Suggested Grades	9–Adult
Guided Tour	None
Maximum Group	50
Group Notice	Arrange in advance
Eating Facilities	None
Restroom Facilities	Yes
Handicapped Access	No

Additional Information Please call (212) 989-5566 for directions.
*Mailing address: P.O. Box 1286,
Bridgehampton, NY 11932 or contact Sarah R. Thompson, Public Affairs, DIA Center for the Arts, 542 West 22nd St., New York, NY 10011 (212) 293-5518.

Kayak and Canoe the Carmans River (Glacier Bay Sports)

GLACIER BAY SPORTS offers kayak and canoe trips along the Carmans River. The upper river trip which runs through the upper Carmans River begins 1/10 of a mile north of the L.I.E. The river flows south through the Southaven County Park. The park is one of the most pristine and natural settings on Long Island. The park offers an almost Appalachian type setting, with green vegetation, trees and a number of rare birds. The trip ends behind our shop where you can end the adventure or continue down river through the Wertheim National Wildlife Refuge. Group trips welcome. Picnic area and restroom available at our shop. Glacier Bay Sports is licensed by Suffolk County as the only kayak and canoe operator on the Carmans River, which flows through the Southaven County Park. Fully insured.

Address/Telephone 2979 Montauk Highway
Brookhaven, NY 11719
(631) 286-0567

When to Visit March 31 to November 15
Monday to Friday—9:00 a.m. to 5:00 p.m.
Saturday and Sunday—8:00 a.m. to 5:00 p.m.

Charges/Fees Call for rates for canoe or kayak
Call for group rates
Reservation required for group (call for information)

Suggested Grades K–Adult—adequate supervision mandatory

Guided Tour Map of river provided
Guides are available at additional cost

Maximum Group Call for information

Group Notice 48 hours

Eating Facilities Picnic area and vending machines

Restroom Facilities Yes

Handicapped Access No

Additional Information Life jackets and paddles provided
A-Trip: Leave car at South Haven Park Terminus, transport of Lower Lake.
B-Trip: Leave car at Glacier Bay Sports and paddle through Wertheim Refuge.

Skydive Long Island

SKYDIVE LONG ISLAND opened its doors in 1986 as the only Student Parachute Center or "Drop Zone" on Long Island. The best-kept secret in America according to the "U.S. Department of Gravity," Skydive Long Island is a member of the United States Parachute Association and employs only certified jumpmasters and instructors. First-time students will do a Tandem Skydive with an instructor, and will receive a Tandem First Jump Certificate. After the Tandem Skydive, students can then take the Static Line First Jump Course, which provides complete instructions for the first solo jump.

Address/Telephone Calverton Airport
4062 Grumman Boulevard
Calverton, NY 11933
(631) 208-3900

Website www.skydivelongisland.com

When to Visit April to November
Tuesday to Friday—9:30 a.m. to sunset
Saturday and Sunday—8:00 a.m. to sunset

Charges/Fees $225.00—first jump (tandem)
$185.00—course (after first tandem jump)
$80.00—post-training jumps
Call for group rates

Suggested Grades Adults (18 and over)

Maximum Group	30
Group Notice	2 weeks
Eating Facilities	Yes, nearby
Restroom Facilities	Yes
Handicapped Access	No
Additional Information	Jumpers must be under 225 pounds

Haven's House

THE HAVEN'S HOUSE, which serves as the headquarters for the Moriches Bay Historical Society, was first built in 1740. Essentially a farmhouse, a Victorian section was added in 1900. The museum displays many items of local memorabilia, Indian artifacts, military medals and 19th-century clothing. Also located at the Haven's House is a library containing various volumes on local and Long Island history.

Address/Telephone	*Montauk Highway and Chet Sweezy Road Center Moriches, NY 11934 (631) 878-1776
When to Visit	Saturday 10:00 a.m. to 5:00 p.m. Groups by appointment
Charges/Fees	None
Suggested Grades	3–Adult
Guided Tour	Yes, 1 hour
Maximum Group	25
Group Notice	1 week
Eating Facilities	None
Restroom Facilities	Emergency only
Handicapped Access	No
Additional Information	*Mailing address: P.O. Box 31, Center Moriches, NY 11934

The 1730 Suydam Homestead and Barn Museum
(Greenlawn-Centerport Historical Association)

THE RESTORED SUYDAM Homestead is now open to visitors. The West Wing Gallery features an exhibit of 18th- and 19th-century redware, pearlware, early creamware and stoneware found during the restoration. The Barn Museum contains a farm workshop, farm wagons and farm implements on exhibit. The upstairs gallery displays home furnishings, including quilts from 19th-century houses in the Greenlawn-Centerport area.

Address/Telephone	*1 Fort Salonga Road
	Centerport, NY 11721
	(631) 754-1180
	Email: gcha-info@usa.net
Website	http://gcha.suffolk.lib.ny.us
When to Visit	Sunday
	June to October
	1:00 p.m. to 4:00 p.m.
Charges/Fees	None
Suggested Grades	4–Adult
Guided Tour	Yes, call 754-1180 for further information
Maximum Group	25
Group Notice	3 weeks
Eating Facilities	None
Restroom Facilities	Yes
Handicapped Access	Barn—Upstairs Gallery not accessible
	Suydam Homestead—partially accessible
	*Mailing address: Box 354, Greenlawn, NY 11740

Vanderbilt Mansion and Marine Museum

THIS 43-ACRE ESTATE, with gardens, Spanish-style mansion, museum and planetarium, overlooks picturesque Northport Harbor and Long Island Sound. Given to Suffolk County by William K. Vanderbilt II, it contains original furnishings from the Vanderbilt years, including carved

Vanderbilt Mansion and Marine Museum　　　　OSCAR SHOENFELD

marble and wood fireplaces, elaborate ceilings and marble-clad galleries. Also on display are wildlife dioramas and exhibits of science and natural history created by Mr. Vanderbilt with collections from his family's travel to exotic places. The Marine Museum is a separate building that houses over 2,000 specimens of marine biology.

Address/Telephone Little Neck Road
　　　　　　　　　Centerport, NY 11721
　　　　　　　　　(631) 854-5555

Website www.vanderbiltmuseum.org

When to Visit Open all year
　　　　　　　September to June
　　　　　　　Tuesday to Sunday—Noon to 5:00 p.m.

July and August
Tuesday to Friday—10:00 a.m. to 5:00 p.m.
Saturday and Sunday—Noon to 5:00 p.m.
Also open Monday holidays—Noon to 5:00 p.m.

Charges/Fees	Grounds pass: Adults—$5.00; students and seniors—$3.00; children under 12—$1.00 House Tour: additional $3.00
Suggested Grades	K–Adult for grounds pass, 6–Adult for house tour
Guided Tour	Yes, 1 hour
Maximum Group	By arrangement; call (631) 854-5568
Group Notice	1 week
Eating Facilities	Outdoor picnic area
Restroom Facilities	Yes
Handicapped Access	No
Additional Information	Gift shop

Vanderbilt Planetarium

THE VANDERBILT PLANETARIUM is one of the largest and best equipped in the United States. A visitor can see the stars, moon, sun and planets displayed on the 60-foot dome by a sophisticated Goto Projector. Rainstorms, 3-D graphics, meteor showers, planetary landscapes and a vast array of special effects entertain young and old alike. State-of-the-art computer automation makes the shows better than ever. Observing sessions are held Friday nights, weather permitting.

Address/Telephone	180 Little Neck Road Centerport, NY 11721 (631) 854-5555
Website	www.vanderbiltmuseum.org
When to Visit	Year-round; call for schedule
Charges/Fees	Adults—$8.00; students and seniors—$6.00; children under 12—$4.00 (Friday night shows—$5.00, $4.00 & $2.50)

Suggested Grades	K–Adult
Guided Tour	None
Maximum Group	238
Group Notice	Varies with program—call at least 1 week in advance
Eating Facilities	Outdoor picnic area
Restroom Facilities	Yes
Handicapped Access	Yes
Additional Information	Observe the rules and regulations. No cameras in the planetarium. Written information available on request.

Long Island Greenbelt Trails

THE LONG ISLAND Greenbelt Trails consist of three major trails extending north to south. The L.I. Trail extends 34 miles from the Great South Bay to the Long Island Sound. The Nassau-Suffolk Trail extends over 20 miles from Cold Spring Harbor to the Massapequa Preserve. The Pine Barrens Trail is a 47-mile route beginning at Rocky Point and ending in Hampton Bays. Group hikes are run throughout the year by the L.I. Greenbelt Trail Conference, but the trails may be used at any time by those who enjoy nature walking. We also operate a "Handicapped Accessible Trail," located behind our Trails Information Center in Manorville.

Address/Telephone	Long Island Greenbelt Trail Conference, Inc. 23 Deer Path Road Central Islip, NY 11722-3404 (631) 360-0753
Website	www.hike-li.com
When to Visit	Daily—dawn to dusk
Charges/Fees	Parking fee at State and County parks in summer
Suggested Grades	K–Adult
Guided Tour	Guided hikes generally on weekends. Call for schedule and places of hikes.

Maximum Group	By arrangement
Group Notice	Call for permission at least one day in advance, especially when hiking through State and County parks.
Eating Facilities	Picnicking, snack bars at Terminus parks and Hidden Pond Park
Restroom Facilities	At State, County and Town parks
Handicapped Access	Lakeland County Park, Caleb Smith State Park, El's Trail in Manorville
Additional Information	Maps ($4.00 each) and guided hike information is available at our Greenbelt Office, (631) 360-0753; or at the Trails Information Center (open April through October, Friday to Monday only), (631) 369-9768; or visit us on the web at www.hike-li.com.

Cold Spring Harbor Whaling Museum

THIS MUSEUM'S ROOMS are filled with hundreds of items evoking memories of the whaling era, including a fully rigged whale boat, scrimshaw, whaling tools and a diorama of Cold Spring Harbor in its whaling port days. The museum offers programs and workshops in scrimshaw, crafts and sea chanteys and a "hands-on" whalebone display. There are special events scheduled on Sunday afternoons. Call for schedule of events.

Address/Telephone	*Main Street (Route 25A) Cold Spring Harbor, NY 11724 (631) 367-3418
Website	www.cshwhalingmuseum.org
When to Visit	Daily (Memorial Day to Labor Day) Tuesday to Sunday (September to May) 11:00 a.m. to 5:00 p.m.
Charges/Fees	Adults—$3.00; seniors—$2.00; students (5–12)— $1.50; children under 5—free

Suggested Grades	Pre-K–Adult
Guided Tour	By arrangement (1 hour with slides or film presentation)
Maximum Group	30 (school groups can be larger)
Group Notice	1 month
Eating Facilities	None
Restroom Facilities	Yes
Handicapped Access	Yes
Additional Information	*Mailing address: P.O. Box 25, Cold Spring Harbor, NY 11724

Dolan DNA Learning Center
(Cold Spring Harbor Laboratory)

THE DOLAN DNA LEARNING CENTER (DNALC) is the educational arm of the Cold Spring Harbor Laboratory. A new museum exhibit focusing on the human genome is scheduled to premiere in June 2002. The exhibit will showcase an 8-foot adaptation of the original 1953 Watson and Crick DNA model, and feature other interactive areas. *Long Island Discovery,* Cablevision's multimedia presentation on Long Island's history and heritage, is shown at 10:00 a.m., 11:00 a.m. and 3:00 p.m., Monday through Friday, and at 1:00 p.m. and 3:00 p.m. on Saturdays. Summer showtimes mid-June through August are 1:00 p.m. and 3:00 p.m., Monday through Saturday. The DNALC hosts a Saturday learning program, and summer workshops for students and teachers.

Address/Telephone	334 Main Street
	Cold Spring Harbor, NY 11724
	(516) 367-5170
	Email: dnalc@cshl.org
Website	www.dnalc.org
When to Visit	Monday to Friday
	10:00 a.m. to 4:00 p.m.
	Saturday—Noon to 4:00 p.m.
	Closed Sundays and holidays

Charges/Fees None for museum exhibit and *Long Island Discovery*.
Call for information about workshop and
Saturday learning program fees.

Suggested Grades 4–Adult

Guided Tour Self-guided

Maximum Group By arrangement

Group Notice 2 weeks

Eating Facilities Lunchroom available; no vending machines or
cafeteria service.

Restroom Facilities Yes

Handicapped Access Yes

Additional Information Educational programs available for middle and
high schools. Call for information.

Dolan DNA Learning Center

The Gallery
(Society for the Preservation of Long Island Antiquities)

L OCATED AT ONE end of the picturesque Village of Cold Spring Harbor, the Gallery provides an opportunity through changing exhibitions to explore aspects of Long Island's distinctive social and cultural history. The Gallery's Museum Shop features an excellent collection of books and objects related to Long Island.

Address/Telephone	*Main Street and Shore Road Cold Spring Harbor, NY 11724 (631) 692-4664
Website	www.splia.org
When to Visit	Saturday and Sunday (January 1 to April 30) 11:00 a.m. to 5:00 p.m. Tuesday to Sunday (May 1 to October 31) 11:00 a.m. to 5:00 p.m. Friday, Saturday and Sunday (November 1 to December 31) 11:00 a.m. to 5:00 p.m.
Charges/Fees	None
Suggested Grades	2–Adult
Guided Tour	Available by appointment
Maximum Group	By arrangement
Group Notice	2 weeks
Eating Facilities	None
Restroom Facilities	Yes
Handicapped Access	Yes
Additional Information	Brochure available. *Mailing address: SPLIA—Society for the Preservation of Long Island Antiquities, 161 Main Street, P.O. Box 148, Cold Spring Harbor, NY 11724

Uplands Farm Sanctuary
(The Nature Conservancy)

T HE HEADQUARTERS OF the Long Island Chapter of The Nature Conservancy, this area of open fields, ash and oak hedgerows, upland woods and farm buildings is also home for the Uplands Farm Sanctuary. Maintained trails in the Sanctuary are open for hiking from dawn till dusk, Monday to Sunday.

Address/Telephone	250 Lawrence Hill Road Cold Spring Harbor, NY 11724 (631) 367-3225 or (631) 367-3384
When to Visit	Monday to Friday—9:00 a.m. to 5:00 p.m. (Office hours) Monday to Sunday—sunrise to sunset (Trail use only)
Charges/Fees	None
Suggested Grades	All ages
Guided Tour	Self-guided trails
Maximum Group	50, with adequate supervision
Group Notice	2 weeks
Eating Facilities	None
Restroom Facilities	Yes, during office hours only (Monday–Friday, 9:00 a.m. to 5:00 p.m.)
Handicapped Access	No
Additional Information	The Nature Conservancy also has offices in East Hampton and on Shelter Island, as well as 13 additional preserves island-wide, which are open to the public. Contact Uplands Farm for more information or preserve guides.

Hoyt Farm Nature Preserve
(Town of Smithtown)

T HE HOYT FARM Nature Preserve is a 136-acre multiple-use park and wildlife preserve. A nature trail with 33 stops has been designed to show all of the habitats and their inhabitants that are to be found at the

Farm. A nature center offers exhibits on the natural history of Long Island. A section of the Hoyt house is devoted to a historical museum featuring furniture and artifacts representing late 18th-century through early 20th-century rural life on Long Island. Visitors will also find a farm animal complex with live animals.

Address/Telephone	New Highway Commack, NY 11725 (631) 543-7804
When to Visit	Memorial Day to September Hoyt House: Saturday and Sunday—2:00 p.m. to 5:00 p.m. Nature Preserve: Daily—1:00 p.m. to 4:00 p.m. Park: All year—8:00 a.m. to dusk School and youth groups by appointment only
Charges/Fees	Fee for educational programs only
Suggested Grades	1–Adult
Guided Tour	Program and tour, 1½ hours
Maximum Group	30
Group Notice	2 weeks
Eating Facilities	Picnic facilities
Restroom Facilities	Yes
Handicapped Access	Limited handicapped facilities available
Additional Information	Environmental education programs by arrangement throughout the year. Parking for Smithtown residents only; others by arrangement.

Telephone Pioneers Museum
(Paumanok Chapter of the Telephone Pioneers of America Historical Museum)

THIS MUSEUM HOUSES nearly 150 phones of all shapes and sizes. In addition, there are nine display units, each with internal lighting and a taped message depicting such things as a lineman explaining how he does the wiring on a telephone pole and a handcrank phone that narrates its

Telephone Pioneers Museum

history. The museum also contains a rare letter written by Thomas Watson (Bell's co-worker), plus a collection of old telephone directories and an 1893 telephone annual report.

Address/Telephone 445 Commack Road
Commack, NY 11725
(631) 543-1321

When to Visit Daily—9:30 a.m. to 4:00 p.m. (By appointment only)
First Sunday of each month—1:00 p.m. to 4:00 p.m. (open house, no appointment needed)

Charges/Fees None

Suggested Grades 2–Adult

Guided Tour	Yes, 1 hour
Maximum Group	50, with 4 adults
Group Notice	2 weeks
Eating Facilities	None
Restroom Facilities	Yes
Handicapped Access	Yes

Bedell Cellars

VISITORS TO BEDELL Cellars sample world-class Merlot, Chardonnay and Cabernet Sauvignon wines in our newly renovated tasting room. Enjoy views of the vineyard and parts of our winery processes.

Address/Telephone	Main Road (Route 25)
	Cutchogue, NY 11935
	(631) 734-7537
Website	www.bedellcellars.com
When to Visit	Daily
	11:00 a.m. to 5:00 p.m.
Charges/Fees	None
Suggested Grades	K–Adult
Guided Tour	By appointment
Maximum Group	Call for information
Group Notice	1 week
Eating Facilities	Picnic facilities available
Restroom Facilities	Yes
Handicapped Access	Yes

Bidwell Vineyards

SITUATED IN THE heart of Long Island wine country, Bidwell Vineyards has distinguished itself by producing a number of award-winning wines. Five specific varieties of grapes are grown to produce seven types of wine. Tours and tasting experiences are available.

Address/Telephone	Route 48 Cutchogue, NY 11935 (631) 734-5200
When to Visit	Daily 11:00 a.m. to 6:00 p.m. Winter: 11:00 a.m. to 5:00 p.m. Tours on weekends only
Charges/Fees	$1.00 per person tasting fee (refundable with any purchase)
Suggested Grades	9–Adult
Guided Tour	Yes
Maximum Group	100
Group Notice	2 weeks
Eating Facilities	Picnic facilities
Restroom Facilities	Yes
Handicapped Access	Yes
Additional Information	Call for special events and program calendar

Castello di Borghese/Hargrave Vineyard

CASTELLO DI BORGHESE/HARGRAVE VINEYARD is the "founding" vineyard of the Long Island wine industry and continues to produce award-winning wines of the highest quality from the region's "oldest" vines. All our wines need is "the pleasure of your company."

Address/Telephone	Route 48 and Alvah's Lane Cutchogue, NY 11935 (631) 734-5111

When to Visit	January to April: 11:00 a.m. to 5:00 p.m. (closed Tuesdays) May to December: Monday to Friday and Sunday— 11:00 a.m. to 5:00 p.m. Saturday—11:00 a.m. to 6:00 p.m.
Charges/Fees	None
Suggested Grades	K-adult
Guided Tour	By appointment only
Maximum Group	30
Group Notice	2 weeks
Eating Facilities	Picnic facilities
Restroom Facilities	Yes
Handicapped Access	Yes
Additional Information	Free wine tasting of selected wines; call for event calendar.

Peconic Bay Winery

PECONIC BAY WINERY is located on the site of a century-old potato farm. Today, this mature grape vineyard produces grapes for five traditional European varieties of wine. The public is invited to daily wine-tasting sessions year-round (closed Tuesdays off-season).

Address/Telephone	Main Road—Route 25 Cutchogue, NY 11935 (631) 734-7361
Website	www.peconicbaywinery.com
When to Visit	Daily 11:00 a.m. to 5:00 p.m. Weekends and holidays 11:00 a.m. to 6:00 p.m.
Charges/Fees	None

Suggested Grades	K–Adult
Guided Tour	By appointment
Maximum Group	20
Group Notice	Call ahead
Eating Facilities	Picnic facilities
Restroom Facilities	Yes
Handicapped Access	Yes
Additional Information	Free wine tastings

Pugliese Vineyards

THIS SMALL VINEYARD offers its visitors free wine-tasting experiences. During the season, demonstrations of wine pressing and a tour of the bottling facility are offered. The vineyards grow three specific grapes to produce a Chardonnay, a Cabernet Sauvignon and a Merlot.

Address/Telephone	Route 25
	Cutchogue, NY 11935
	(631) 734-4057
Website	www.pugliesevineyards.com
When to Visit	Daily
	11:00 a.m. to 5:00 p.m.
Charges/Fees	None
Suggested Grades	K–Adult
Guided Tour	Yes, by appointment
Maximum Group	By arrangement
Group Notice	2 weeks
Eating Facilities	Picnic facilities
Restroom Facilities	Yes
Handicapped Access	Yes

Village Green Complex
(Cutchogue-New Suffolk Historical Council)

THE VILLAGE GREEN Complex, typifying the way of life for over 300 years on these and neighboring farmlands, features The Old House (1649), The Wickham Farm House (c. 1740), the Old School Museum (1840), and the Village Library (1862). The Old House is a registered National Historic Landmark. The School House was Cutchogue's first district school. A mid-19th century carriage house was recently added to the complex.

Address/Telephone	Village Green (Route 25) Cutchogue, NY 11935 (631) 734-7122
When to Visit	Last weekend in June to first weekend in September Tours are from 1:00 p.m. to 4:00 p.m. Groups by appointment
Charges/Fees	None
Suggested Grades	3–Adult
Guided Tour	Yes, 1 hour
Maximum Group	By arrangement
Group Notice	2 weeks
Eating Facilities	Picnic facilities
Restroom Facilities	Yes
Handicapped Access	No
Additional Information	Various Saturday programs throughout the summer.

Willow Pet Hotel

THE WILLOW PET Hotel is the largest, most modern pet-boarding facility on the East Coast. Both registered and inspected by the Department of Agriculture, this facility is also one of the largest pet-grooming centers in the United States. This same facility operates a unique pet-transportation service, shipping both dogs and cats for relocated owners all over the world. Students will observe grooming operations through a glass window as some 40 to 70 animals are groomed each day. A tour through the cattery and dog-boarding areas will also take place. The Willow Pet Hotel will help all Girl Scouts and Boy Scouts work toward earning their pet/animal care badges.

Address/Telephone	1926 Deer Park Avenue
	Deer Park, NY 11729
	(631) 667-8924 Call: Marc Rosenzweig for tours.
	Email: willowpet@saturn5.net
Website	www.willowpethotel.com
When to Visit	Monday, Tuesday, Thursday, Friday and Saturday
	11:00 a.m. to 3:00 p.m.
Charges/Fees	None
Suggested Grades	3–9
Guided Tour	Yes, 15 to 30 minutes
Maximum Group	35, with one adult per group of 10
Group Notice	2 weeks
Eating Facilities	None
Restroom Facilities	Yes
Handicapped Access	No
Additional Information	Children should not touch the cages.

Adventureland
(Long Island's Amusement Park)

As an amusement park, Adventureland provides some of the latest rides and special attractions found in theme parks around the nation. In terms of video and entertaining games, it has been described as a veritable warehouse of games. As a restaurant and eating establishment, Adventureland remains a legend on Long Island for its great hot dogs, deli sandwiches and pizza.

Address/Telephone	2245 Route 110
	East Farmingdale, NY 11735
	(631) 694-6868
Website	www.adventurelandfamilyfun.com
When to Visit	Park Season—April to October
	Restaurant and Game Room—All year
Charges/Fees	Call for information and group rates
Suggested Grades	Pre-K–Adult
Guided Tour	None
Maximum Group	Unlimited
Group Notice	None
Eating Facilities	Yes
Restroom Facilities	Yes
Handicapped Access	Yes

Republic Airport

R EPUBLIC AIRPORT, EAST Farmingdale, provides educational and fun tours for children, adults and organizations. The tour consists of a visit to the Control Tower and the Crash/Fire/Rescue Operations. At the Control Tower visitors are able to observe the FAA air traffic controllers conducting conversations with pilots and other air traffic control centers.

Address/Telephone	7150 Republic Airport
	East Farmingdale, NY 11735
	(631) 752-7707 Call: Operations Manager
Website	www.republicairport.net
When to Visit	Monday to Friday
	10:00 a.m. to 11:00 p.m.
	Tours by appointment only
Charges/Fees	None
Suggested Grades	1–Adult

Guided Tour	Yes, 1 hour
Maximum Group	15
Group Notice	6 months
Eating Facilities	Picnic facilities and vending machines available
Restroom Facilities	Yes
Handicapped Access	Yes
Additional Information	Trips to tower depend on operational considerations.

Clinton Academy
(East Hampton Historical Society)

CLINTON ACADEMY, THE first academy chartered in New York State, served as a college preparatory school from 1784 to 1881 and later as a community center. It is now a museum that presents major interpretive exhibits from the East Hampton Historical Society's collections. There is also a collection of textiles, tools and equipment relating to local and regional history. Guided tours and classes are available.

Address/Telephone	*151 Main Street East Hampton, NY 11937 (631) 324-1850 or (631) 324-6850
When to Visit	July and August—1:00 p.m. to 5:00 p.m. Spring/Fall weekends and by appointment Groups call for appointment during summer and winter months
Charges/Fees	Public: Adults—$4.00; children and seniors—$2.00 Schools: call for arrangements
Suggested Grades	Pre-K–Adult
Guided Tour	Gallery talks
Maximum Group	40, with adequate supervision
Group Notice	2 weeks
Eating Facilities	None

Restroom Facilities Yes

Handicapped Access Limited

Additional Information Call for information on a variety of school programs. Recommended: combined tour of Clinton Academy and Town House Museum.

*Mailing address: 101 Main Street, East Hampton, NY 11937

(631) 324-6850

Guild Hall Museum

G UILD HALL IS an art museum with a permanent collection of 1,800 paintings, sculpture and works on paper by the major artists associated with the region, including Lee Krasner, Jimmy Ernst, Willem de Kooning, Childe Hassam, Thomas Moran and others. The schedule of contemporary art exhibitions continues year-round with a student arts festival members show as well as group and solo exhibitions of nationally known artists. Guild Hall also includes the John Drew Theater.

Address/Telephone 158 Main Street
East Hampton, NY 11937
(631) 324-0806
Email: pr@guildhall.org

Website www.guildhall.org

When to Visit Fall to Spring:
Thursday to Saturday—11:00 a.m. to 5:00 p.m.
Sunday—Noon to 5:00 p.m.
Summer:
Daily—11:00 a.m. to 5:00 p.m.
Sunday—Noon to 5:00 p.m.

Charges/Fees Members—free; non-members—$4.00

Suggested Grades K–Adult

Guided Tour Yes, by arrangement

Maximum Group 60 (30 for guided tour)

Group Notice	2 weeks
Eating Facilities	None
Restroom Facilities	Yes
Handicapped Access	Yes
Additional Information	Write or call for calendar of events or summer theater brochure

Home Sweet Home Museum

THIS 18TH-CENTURY SALTBOX house is dedicated to the memory of John Howard Payne, author of over 70 plays and a champion for the American copyright laws. He was also a champion of the rights of Native Americans and author of the poem "Home Sweet Home." The house is filled with furnishings from three centuries of East Hampton's history. The 1804 Pantigo Windmill, a fine example of early wooden technology, is located on the property.

Address/Telephone	14 James Lane East Hampton, NY 11937 (631) 324-0713
When to Visit	Monday to Saturday—10:00 a.m. to 4:00 p.m. Sunday—2:00 p.m. to 4:00 p.m.
Charges/Fees	Adults—$4.00; children—$2.00
Suggested Grades	4–Adult
Guided Tour	Yes, for all visitors
Maximum Group	By arrangement
Group Notice	1 week
Eating Facilities	None
Restroom Facilities	None
Handicapped Access	No

John Drew Theater of Guild Hall

THE HISTORIC JOHN DREW Theater of Guild Hall seats 400 for musical and dramatic productions, lectures, readings, films, dance recitals and concerts. Productions continue throughout the year and the theater offers a variety of educational programming to enhance appreciation and make the arts accessible to a broad audience.

Address/Telephone	158 Main Street
	East Hampton, NY 11937
	(631) 324-0806
	Box office: (631) 324-4050
	Email: pr@guildhall.org
Website	www.guildhall.org
When to Visit	Programs scheduled all year.
	Call for latest times and dates.
Charges/Fees	Varies with program.
	Group discounts available.
Suggested Grades	K–Adult
Guided Tour	None
Group Notice	2 weeks
Eating Facilities	None
Restroom Facilities	Yes
Handicapped Access	Yes
Additional Information	Infra-red hearing system for the hearing-impaired. Young People Theater Workshops and Summer Apprenticeship programs available.

Long Island Collection
(East Hampton Library)

THIS COLLECTION OF books, pamphlets, maps, newspapers, genealogies and government documents relating to the history and people of Long Island was originally donated by Morton Pannypacker. The Thomas Moran Biographical Art Collection and The Seversmith Collection (books and artifacts used in compiling his book on Colonial families of the region) are among the materials available, as well as special indexes to historical records.

Address/Telephone	159 Main Street
	East Hampton, NY 11937
	(631) 324-0222
	Fax: (631) 329-7184
	Email: ehamlib@suffolk.lib.ny.us
Website	www.easthamptonlibrary.org
When to Visit	Monday to Saturday
	1:00 p.m. to 4:30 p.m.
	Morning hours available by appointment
Charges/Fees	None
Suggested Grades	4–Adult
Guided Tour	None
Maximum Group	15
Group Notice	2 weeks
Eating Facilities	None
Restroom Facilities	Yes
Handicapped Access	Ramp to main library for handicapped

Merrill Lake Sanctuary
(The Nature Conservancy)

THE SANCTUARY HOSTS an exemplary accessible salt-marsh community, with both low and high marsh zones. Largely covered with plant life, at high tide the marsh is sometimes flooded with salt water. It also serves as a nursery for fish and wildlife. There is a self-guided trail with an explanatory booklet illustrating plants and wildlife found at the salt marsh. There are several nesting osprey at the Sanctuary.

Address/Telephone *Springs Fire Place Road and Hog Creek Road
East Hampton, NY 11937
Office: (631) 329-7689

Website www.nature.org/southfork

When to Visit Daily
Sunrise to sunset

Charges/Fees None

Suggested Grades K–Adult

Guided Tour Yes, 60 to 90 minutes—2 weeks notice needed

Maximum Group 20

Group Notice 4 weeks

Eating Facilities None

Restroom Facilities None

Handicapped Access No

Additional Information Talk may be arranged at main office,
call (631) 329-7689.
*Mailing address: The Nature Conservancy,
South Fork-Shelter Island Chapter,
P.O. Box 5125, East Hampton, NY 11937

The Mulford Farm c. 1790 House and Barn and Award-Winning Rachel's Garden (East Hampton Historical Society)

THE MULFORD FARM is a living history, hands-on museum site. The house dates from 1680 and was maintained by one family for eight generations. It is interpreted as both a period house and architectural site. It displays furniture and farm implements that help tell the history of a community and a family that lived and worked there. The barn, built in 1721, serves as a programming area.

Address/Telephone	*10 James Lane East Hampton, NY 11937 (631) 324-6864 or (631) 324-6850
When to Visit	July and August—1:00 p.m. to 5:00 p.m. Spring/Fall weekends and by appointment Groups call for appointment during summer and winter months.
Charges/Fees	Public: Adults—$4.00; children and seniors—$2.00 Schools: call for arrangements
Suggested Grades	Pre-K–Adult
Guided Tour	Costumed interpreter/living history demonstrations
Maximum Group	40+, with adequate supervision
Group Notice	2 weeks
Eating Facilities	Picnic facilities
Restroom Facilities	Yes
Handicapped Access	Yes
Additional Information	Call for information on a variety of school programs. *Mailing address: 101 Main Street, East Hampton, NY 11937 (631) 324-6850

Old Hook Mill

TODAY EAST HAMPTON features the greatest concentration of windmills to be found anywhere in the United States. Old Hook Mill, built in 1806 by Nathaniel Dominy, is one of four mills located within the Village of East Hampton. The mill was refurbished and put into operating condition in 1939. Guided tours are given to all visitors.

Address/Telephone	*Montauk Highway East Hampton, NY 11937 (631) 324-0713
When to Visit	June, July and August Weekdays—10:00 a.m. to 4:00 p.m. Sunday—2:00 p.m. to 4:00 p.m.

Charges/Fees Adults—$2.00; children—$1.00

Suggested Grades 2–Adult

Guided Tour Yes

Maximum Group 5

Group Notice 1 week

Eating Facilities None

Restroom Facilities None

Handicapped Access No

Additional Information *Mailing address: 14 James Lane, East Hampton, NY 11937
Bus tours by appointment.
Souvenirs on premises.

Osborn-Jackson House
(East Hampton Historical Society)

THE OSBORN-JACKSON HOUSE, dating from c. 1740, is one of the few remaining 18th-century houses in place on Main Street. The house is interpreted as the 19th-century period home of Slyvanus Mulford Osborn, utilizing Dominy furniture and decorative art pieces from the Society's collection. The house also serves as the Society's administrative offices.

Address/Telephone 101 Main Street
East Hampton, NY 11937
(631) 324-6850

When to Visit Monday to Friday—Year-round
10:00 a.m. to 5:00 p.m.

Charges/Fees Adults—$4.00; children and seniors—$2.00

Suggested Grades K–Adult

Guided Tour By appointment

Maximum Group 20, with adequate supervision

Group Notice 2 weeks

Eating Facilities None

Restroom Facilities	Yes
Handicapped Access	Limited
Additional Information	Visit this site in conjunction with Clinton Academy and Town House Museum.

Pollock Krasner House and Study Center

T HIS HOUSE IS the former home and studio of the Abstract Expressionist painters Jackson Pollock and Lee Krasner, his wife. The Center's purposes are to preserve and interpret the site, which is highlighted by the paint-spattered floor on which Pollock created many of his masterpieces; and to provide facilities for research on 20th-century American art, with special emphasis on the artists' community of eastern Long Island. In addition to guided tours of the site, the program includes art exhibitions, lectures and special events during the summer season.

Address/Telephone	830 Fireplace Road East Hampton, NY 11937 (631) 324-4929
When to Visit	Open for guided tours by appointment Thursday, Friday and Saturday May to October 11:00 a.m. to 4:00 p.m. Study Center research collections open by appointment year-round.
Charges/Fees	Admission—$5.00 (lecture and special event tickets vary in price)
Suggested Grades	Pre-K–Adult
Guided Tour	By appointment, 45 minutes to 1 hour
Maximum Group	40
Group Notice	Individuals and small groups—1 week Bus tours and other large groups—1 month
Eating Facilities	None
Restroom Facilities	Yes
Handicapped Access	House

Town House Museum
(East Hampton Historical Society)

THIS FACILITY SERVED as the first town-meeting hall and schoolhouse. Originally located on the north end common, it was moved to three other locations before its final site next to Clinton Academy. The Town House was opened in summer 1989, providing visitors with an interactive East Hampton 18th century living-history "class", presented by a costumed interpreter.

Address/Telephone	*149 Main Street East Hampton, NY 11937 (631) 324-6850
When to Visit	July and August—1:00 p.m. to 5:00 p.m. Spring/Fall weekends and by appointment Groups call for appointment during summer and winter months.
Charges/Fees	Public: Adults—$4.00; children and seniors—$2.00 Schools: Call for arrangements
Suggested Grades	Pre-K–Adult
Guided Tour	Yes, living history class, approximately 1 hour
Maximum Group	20, with adequate supervision
Group Notice	2 weeks
Eating Facilities	None
Restroom Facilities	None
Handicapped Access	Limited
Additional Information	Call for information on a variety of school programs. *Mailing address: 101 Main Street, East Hampton, NY 11937

BroadHollow Theatres

THE BROADHOLLOW THEATRE Company, a not-for-profit arts organization, lights up three stages on Long Island with theatres located in Rockville Centre, Lindenhurst and East Islip. The company produces both mainstage and children's shows as well as educational plays for school groups. Mainstage productions offer weekend, evening and matinee performances; children's theatre is performed on Saturday afternoons. School and youth groups are booked by appointment.

Address/Telephone Mailing address:
265 East Main Street, Suite 162
East Islip, NY 11730
(631) 581-2700

Theatre locations:
Centre Stage at Molloy College
1000 Hempstead Avenue
Rockville Centre, NY 11570

Studio Theatre
141 South Wellwood Avenue
Lindenhurst, NY 11757

BayWay Arts Center
265 East Main Street
East Islip, NY 11730

Website www.broadhollow.org

When to Visit Children's shows: Saturday—call for schedule
Mainstage: Friday, Saturday and Sunday—call for schedule
School and youth groups: Monday to Friday—call for appointment

Charges/Fees Call for information

Suggested Grades Pre-K–Adult, depending on program

Guided Tour None

Maximum Group 175

Group Notice General public—1 week. Groups over 10—2 to 3 weeks.

Eating Facilities None

Restroom Facilities Yes

Handicapped Access Yes (except for Studio Theatre)

Additional Information Call for up-to-date information on programs and fees.

Islip Art Museum

T HE ISLIP ART MUSEUM is the leading exhibition space for contemporary art on Long Island. Changing exhibits focus on themes and concerns of the current art world. Tours provide good introduction to the visual arts and are geared to school groups. The museum also provides teacher-education workshops.

Address/Telephone	50 Irish Lane East Islip, NY 11730 (631) 224-5402 Fax: (631) 224-5440
Website	www.islipartmuseum.org
When to Visit	School groups by appointment
Charges/Fees	Donation
Suggested Grades	3–12
Guided Tour	Yes
Maximum Group	30, with adequate supervision
Group Notice	2 weeks minimum
Eating Facilities	None
Restroom Facilities	Yes
Handicapped Access	Yes
Additional Information	The museum operates The Carriage House on a seasonal schedule beginning in May. Experimental, site-specific and over-sized works are featured. The museum also provides "packages" for school groups, which include visits to the nearby South Shore Nature Center and/or Town Hall. Call for information.

South Shore Nature Center
(Town of Islip)

THIS NATURE CENTER represents one of the few areas left on Long Island where an ecological balance between uplands, freshwater swamp and salt marsh has been preserved. It is situated on 200 acres. Visitors can walk its 2½ miles of nature trails with the aid of a guidebook or take one of the many special-subject guided walks offered at the center, where there is also a small natural history museum. There is also an instructional program available.

Address/Telephone	*Bayview Avenue East Islip, NY 11730 (631) 224-5436
When to Visit	Daily—April to October Monday to Friday—November to March 9:00 a.m. to 5:00 p.m.
Charges/Fees	None (Call for schedule of program fees)
Suggested Grades	Pre-K–Adult
Guided Tour	By arrangement
Maximum Group	30, with adequate supervision
Group Notice	2 weeks
Eating Facilities	Picnic facilities
Restroom Facilities	Yes
Handicapped Access	Yes
Additional Information	*Mailing address: South Shore Nature Center, 50 Irish Lane, East Islip, NY 11730

Swan River Schoolhouse Museum

THE SWAN RIVER Schoolhouse, built in 1858, was last used as a school in 1936. Now a museum, this former one-room schoolhouse shows typical school furniture, the original schoolhouse bell and books used by the students who attended this school.

Address/Telephone	*Roe Avenue East Patchogue, NY 11772 (631) 475-1700
When to Visit	Tuesday, Thursday and Friday—by appointment
Charges/Fees	None
Suggested Grades	K–8
Guided Tour	Yes, about 15 minutes
Maximum Group	30
Group Notice	1 week
Eating Facilities	None
Restroom Facilities	None
Handicapped Access	Yes
Additional Information	*Mailing address: David A. Overton, Brookhaven Town Historian, 3233 Route 112, Medford, NY 11763 (631) 654-7897

Sherwood-Jayne House
(Society for the Preservation of Long Island Antiquities)

THIS SALTBOX HOUSE is filled with a varied collection of antiques and furnishings, pewter, textiles and paintings. Hand-painted wall frescoes are located in the east parlor and east bedroom and are discussed in major books on early American wall decoration.

Address/Telephone	*55 Old Post Road East Setauket, NY 11733 (631) 692-4664 Call: Society for the Preservation of Long Island Antiquities
Website	www.splia.org
When to Visit	By appointment

Charges/Fees	Adults—$3.00; children and seniors—$1.50 Call for school discovery brochure and fees
Suggested Grades	2–Adult
Guided Tour	Yes, 45 minutes
Maximum Group	By arrangement
Group Notice	2 weeks
Eating Facilities	None
Restroom Facilities	None
Handicapped Access	No
Additional Information	Annual Long Island Apple Festival held last Sunday in September. *Mailing address: SPLIA—Society for the Preservation of Long Island Antiquities, 161 Main Street, P.O. Box 148, Cold Spring Harbor, NY 11724

Barnstable Broadcasting
Long Island Radio Group
(B-103/Island 94.3/WKJY/WHLI)

A T B-103/ISLAND 94.3, visitors will see newscasters and disc jockeys in action on the air. Also observed will be news programs in preparation as well as news service teletype facilities. Also on site are the facilities for WKJY and WHLI.

Address/Telephone	234 Airport Plaza, Second Floor Farmingdale, NY 11735 (631) 770-4200
Websites	www.b103.com; www.island943.com; www.kjoy.com; www.whli.com
When to Visit	By appointment
Charges/Fees	None
Suggested Grades	5–Adult

Guided Tour	Yes, 15 minutes
Maximum Group	15, with adequate supervision
Group Notice	4 weeks
Eating Facilities	None
Restroom Facilities	Yes
Handicapped Access	Yes

Fire Island Coast Guard Station

THIS COAST GUARD station serves as a base for search and rescue operations. A communications center, weather observation post and boats are part of the facility. The tour includes the main building and a close-up view of the boats. Visitors will have a chance to meet the personnel, see and hear the radios in operation and hear an explanation of the rescue process. Other areas of the station's responsibility include Law Enforcement and Marine Pollution Response.

Address/Telephone	*Robert Moses State Park Fire Island (631) 661-9101 Call: Commanding Officer
When to Visit	Monday to Friday 9:00 a.m. to 11:00 a.m. and 1:00 p.m. to 4:00 p.m. Hours depend on current operations and availability of personnel; call for appointment. Group tours only; we cannot accommodate groups under 10 persons, or individuals.
Charges/Fees	None
Suggested Grades	3–Adult
Guided Tour	Yes, 45 minutes to 1 hour
Maximum Group	30, with adequate supervision
Group Notice	1 month advance notice with confirmation is required.
Eating Facilities	None
Restroom Facilities	Yes
Handicapped Access	No
Additional Information	*Mailing address: Commanding Officer, USCG Station Fire Island, Babylon, NY 11702

Fire Island Lighthouse
(Fire Island National Seashore)

L OCATED AT THE western terminus of the National Seashore, the Lighthouse is accessible by automobile via Robert Moses Causeway. Parking is available at Robert Moses State Park Field 5, then walk ¾-mile east to lighthouse. The Visitor Center is open to groups and the general public. The one-mile-long boardwalk trail provides access to both the Great South Bay and ocean beaches.

Address/Telephone	*Fire Island Lighthouse (631) 661-4876
When to Visit	Call (631) 661-4876 for hours.
Charges/Fees	None
Suggested Grades	K–Adult
Guided Tour	By reservation only, 2 hours
Maximum Group	60
Group Notice	2 weeks
Eating Facilities	Nearby at Robert Moses State Park
Restroom Facilities	Yes
Handicapped Access	Yes
Additional Information	Danger: Strong surf and poison ivy. Ticks can cause health problems. *Mailing address: 120 Laurel Street, Patchogue, NY 11772

Sailors Haven
(Fire Island National Seashore)

S AILORS HAVEN, ONE of the Fire Island National Seashore facilities, features the Sunken Forest Nature Trail, marina and visitor center. Sailors Haven is accessible by ferry for passengers only. There are interpretive programs, nature walks, beaches and a restaurant. Sand wheelchairs are available on request.

Address/Telephone	*Sailors Haven Fire Island National Seashore (631) 597-6183—Visitor Center (seasonal) (631) 289-4810—Park Headquarters (year-round)
When to Visit	May to October
Charges/Fees	None
Suggested Grades	K–Adult
Guided Tour	Call (631) 289-4810 for information.
Maximum Group	By arrangement
Group Notice	None
Eating Facilities	Yes
Restroom Facilities	Yes
Handicapped Access	Yes, but limited on nature trails. Sand wheelchairs available on request.
Additional Information	Danger: strong surf. Ticks can cause health problems. Stay on park's boardwalks or on beach to avoid ticks' habitat. For ferry service information, call (631) 589-8980. *Mailing address: 120 Laurel Street, Patchogue, NY 11772

Watch Hill
(Fire Island National Seashore)

WATCH HILL IS located in the eastern portion of the National Seashore Park. It provides 200 boat slips and includes water and electrical hookups. There are also camping facilities available for tents (no charge). A feature of this area of the Seashore is the large saltwater marsh and special nature trails. Watch Hill is adjacent to the only federal Wilderness Area in New York State.

Address/Telephone	*Watch Hill (631) 597-6455

When to Visit	May to October
	9:00 a.m. to 6:00 p.m.
	Visitor Center: Daily, July and August—9:30 a.m.
	to 5:30 p.m.
Charges/Fees	None
Suggested Grades	K–Adult
Guided Tour	Call (631) 289-4810 for information.
Maximum Group	By arrangement
Group Notice	None
Eating Facilities	Picnic facilities. Snack bar and restaurant, call
	(631) 597-6655 for information.
Restroom Facilities	Yes
Handicapped Access	Yes

Watch Hill   NATIONAL PARK SERVICE

Additional Information Danger: Strong surf and poison ivy. Ticks can cause health problems.
Call for current ferry rates and schedule. Davis Park Ferry Company, (631) 475-1665. Camping reservations: (631) 597-6633.
*Mailing address: 120 Laurel Street, Patchogue, NY 11772

Wilderness Visitor Center
(Fire Island National Seashore)

WILDERNESS VISITOR CENTER (formerly Smith Point), the eastern terminus of the National Seashore, is located at the southern end of William Floyd Parkway. A Visitor's Center with exhibits is on location. A trail ⅔ of a mile in length highlights the natural and cultural history of the area. Wilderness Visitor Center is on the easternmost edge of an eight-mile-long federal wilderness area. All parking is adjacent to the Seashore at Smith Point County Park.

Address/Telephone	*Fire Island National Seashore (631) 281-3010
When to Visit	Seashore: Open all year
Charges/Fees	Parking fee at County Park
Suggested Grades	K–Adult
Guided Tour	Orientation programs and Environmental Education Programs—call in advance
Maximum Group	60
Group Notice	2 weeks
Eating Facilities	None
Restroom Facilities	Yes
Handicapped Access	Yes

Additional Information   Danger: Strong surf and poison ivy. Ticks can cause health problems.

No lifeguard on duty. Boardwalk, lavatory and first floor of Visitor Center accessible to handicapped. Park Ranger is available upon request to present interpretive programs to school groups at their school if they cannot make it to Fire Island National Seashore.

*Mailing address: 120 Laurel Street, Patchogue, NY 11772

•

The Big Duck

PERHAPS LONG ISLAND'S most famous landmark, the Big Duck is recognized by architects and historians as one of America's finest examples of "Roadside Architecture." It was donated to Suffolk County in 1987 and has been lovingly restored by the Friends for Long Island's Heritage. The unique structure now serves as an official Long Island tourist information center and a gift shop selling "Duckobelia."

Address/Telephone	*Route 24 Flanders, NY 11901 (631) 852-8292
When to Visit	May 1 to Labor Day 7 days a week—10:00 a.m. to 5:00 p.m. Thanksgiving to Christmas Weekends only—10:00 a.m. to 5:00 p.m.
Charges/Fees	None
Suggested Grades	Pre-K–Adult
Guided Tour	None
Maximum Group	30
Group Notice	None
Eating Facilities	Picnic facilities nearby at Sears Bellows County Park
Restroom Facilities	Nearby at Sears Bellows County Park
Handicapped Access	Yes

Additional Information   No visit to Long Island is complete without a pho-
tograph of the Big Duck. Exterior viewing only.
*Mailing address: Richard C. Martin, c/o Suffolk
County Dept. of Parks, P.O. Box 144, W. Sayville,
NY 11796

Bayard Cutting Arboretum

L OCATED ON 690 acres, this oasis of beauty and quiet contains numerous
trees, shrubs and flower varieties. Many varieties of aquatic and land
birds may be seen. There are several self-guided walks through the
Arboretum. Located in the former Cutting residence are examples of
antique English woodwork and Tiffany glass. Concerts, meetings, classes
and exhibits are presented at the Arboretum.

Address/Telephone   *Montauk Highway
Great River, NY 11739
(631) 581-1002

When to Visit   Year-round—10:00 a.m. to sunset

Charges/Fees   Vehicle use fee: $5.00
Bus: Nonprofit—$25.00; others—$50.00
Effective first Saturday in April to Labor Day—
daily
After Labor Day to last Sunday in October—
weekends only
No winter fees

Suggested Grades   K–Adult

Guided Tour   Yes, by special arrangement

Maximum Group   50 (groups over 50 and buses need permit)

Group Notice   2 weeks

Eating Facilities   Yes, year-round. (Café closed two weeks in
February for maintenance and repairs.)

Restroom Facilities   Yes

Handicapped Access   Yes

Additional Information Every group leader must report to the director's office in the administration building. No food may be brought into the Arboretum from the outside. Manor House is open year-round.
*Mailing address: P.O. Box 466, Oakdale, NY 11769

Greenlawn-Centerport Historical Association Museum

HOUSED IN THE Harborfields Public Library, this museum's office and research center offers a growing collection of photographs, documents, genealogical information, objects and oral and written histories relating to Greenlawn and Centerport. Changing exhibits reflect the histories of the two communities and the lifestyles of the local people. There are demonstrations and educational programs offered by the museum.

Address/Telephone *31 Broadway
Greenlawn, NY 11746
(631) 754-1180
Email: gcha-info@usa.net

Website http://gcha.suffolk.lib.ny.us

When to Visit Tuesday and Thursday—1:00 p.m. to 4:00 p.m.
Monday, Wednesday and Friday—
9:00 a.m. to 1:00 p.m.
Groups call for appointment

Charges/Fees None (donations accepted)

Suggested Grades K–12

Guided Tour Yes, docents on duty Sundays and by appointment

Maximum Group 12

Group Notice 3 weeks

Eating Facilities None

Restroom Facilities Yes

Handicapped Access Yes

Additional Information Located in Harborfields Public Library building. Programs may be designed according to group needs and interests.
*Mailing address: Box 354, Greenlawn, NY 11740

East End Seaport Maritime Museum

L OCATED IN THE historic village of Greenport, the East End Seaport Maritime Museum focuses on the rich maritime heritage of the eastern end of Long Island. The museum's lighthouse exhibit features two rare lighthouse lenses from Little Gull and Plum Island. Other artifacts include ship models and tools, memorabilia from the 1930s America's Cup yacht, *Ranger*, a historical exhibit on the Coastal Pickets of World War II, and an aquarium.

Address/Telephone *Third Street (at the Ferry Dock)
Greenport, NY 11904
(631) 477-2100, (631) 477-0004

When to Visit Memorial Day to Labor Day
Wednesday to Sunday—10:00 a.m. to 5:00 p.m.
May, September and October
Weekends only—10:00 a.m. to 4:00 p.m.

Charges/Fees Free (donations accepted)

Suggested Grades 3–Adult

Guided Tour By appointment

Maximum Group 50

Group Notice 2 weeks

Eating Facilities None

Restroom Facilities Yes

Handicapped Access 1st floor only

Additional Information Gift shop on premises.
*Mailing address: P.O. Box 624, Greenport, NY 11944

Malabar
(Downeast Windjammer Cruises)

BUILT IN 1975 and recently restored by Capt. Steven F. Pagels, the 105-foot two-masted topsail schooner *Malabar* is available for educational and recreational programs. Additionally, the *Malabar* goes out daily on two-hour daysails. Fully certified by the U.S. Coast Guard, the *Malabar* can carry up to 49 passengers on daysails, and 21 passengers overnight. The *Malabar* currently sails from the village of Greenport.

Address/Telephone	*Mitchell Park Greenport, NY 11944 (631) 477-3698
Website	www.downeastwindjammer.com
When to Visit	Mid-May to mid-October
Charges/Fees	Call for information
Suggested Grades	K-Adult
Guided Tour	Call for information
Maximum Group	49
Group Notice	Make arrangements in advance
Eating Facilities	"Brown bag"
Restroom Facilities	Yes
Handicapped Access	No
Additional Information	*Mailing address: P.O. Box 28, Cherryfield, ME 04622

Railroad Museum of Long Island

THE RAILROAD MUSEUM of Long Island (RMLI), the only authentic railroad museum in the New York City/Long Island area, has two operational sites on eastern Long Island. The Greenport site is home to our museum building, which is a restored 1890s LIRR freight depot. Adjacent to the building is a 1907 snowplow and a 1927 LIRR wooden caboose. The Riverhead site houses the bulk of the railroad collection including steam engine #39, which is currently undergoing restoration to working condition.

Address/Telephone	P.O. Box 726
	Greenport, NY 11944
	(631) 477-0439
	Riverhead: (631) 727-7920
When to Visit	Greenport: May to first weekend in December
	Weekends only—Noon to 4:00 p.m.
	Riverhead: Saturdays (weather permitting)
	10:00 a.m. to 4:00 p.m.
Charges/Fees	Donation
Suggested Grades	Pre-K–Adult
Guided Tour	Yes
Maximum Group	40–50
Group Notice	Please call as early as possible.
Eating Facilities	"Brown bag"
Restroom Facilities	Yes (Greenport); Yes (Riverhead)
Handicapped Access	No (Greenport); Limited (Riverhead)

Stirling Historical Society and Museum

THIS 1831 HOMESTEAD serves both as a village museum and the Stirling Historical Society's headquarters. Located in Monsell Park, the Museum is a good place to acquaint oneself with the history of Greenport and then casually walk the quaint streets of the village, which are filled with many early homes. This old fishing, shipbuilding and whaling village saw many famous guests, such as John Quincy Adams, General Winfield Scott and Admiral George Dewey during its earlier days.

Address/Telephone	*Main Street
	Greenport, NY 11944
	(631) 477-3026
When to Visit	Saturday and Sunday and holidays
	July to September
	1:00 p.m. to 4:00 p.m.
Charges/Fees	Donation
Suggested Grades	4–Adult
Guided Tour	Yes, by arrangement

Maximum Group	30
Group Notice	1 week
Eating Facilities	None
Restroom Facilities	None
Handicapped Access	No
Additional Information	*Mailing address: P.O. Box 590, Greenport, NY 11944

Shinnecock Coast Guard Station

THIS COAST GUARD station serves as a base for search and rescue operations. A communications center, weather observation post and boats are part of the facility. The tour includes the main building and a close-up view of the boats. Visitors will have a chance to meet the personnel, see and hear the radios in operation and hear an explanation of the rescue process. Other areas of the station's responsibility include Law Enforcement and Marine Pollution Investigation.

Address/Telephone	100 Foster Avenue Hampton Bays, NY 11946 (631) 728-0078 Call: Operations Officer
When to Visit	Monday to Saturday 9:30 a.m. to 11:30 a.m. and 2:30 p.m. to 4:30 p.m.
Charges/Fees	None
Suggested Grades	Pre-K–12
Guided Tour	Yes, 30 minutes
Maximum Group	25, with one adult per group of 8
Group Notice	1 month
Eating Facilities	None
Restroom Facilities	Yes
Handicapped Access	No

Holtsville Park and Ecology Site
(Town of Brookhaven)

O NCE A GARBAGE dump, this site is now a thriving environmental and educational park. Visitors may walk on hills made from garbage that now have trees and wildflowers growing on them, or may visit a barnyard and native North American animal preserve, home to many permanently injured animals. One can get a close-up look at how leaves are recycled into compost for town residents. This compost is then used to enrich the soil. There is a jogging and exercise trail, swimming pools, picnic area and playground available.

Address/Telephone	249 Buckley Road Holtsville, NY 11742 (631) 758-9664
Website	www.brookhaven.org
When to Visit	Park: Daily—9:00 a.m. to dusk Animal Preserve: Daily—9:00 a.m. to 4:00 p.m.
Charges/Fees	None (except for fee at pools)
Suggested Grades	1–Adult
Guided Tour	Yes, 1½ hour tour, including talk on problems of resource recovery, endangered species and wild-life habitats
Maximum Group	50
Group Notice	2 weeks to 6 months, depending on season
Eating Facilities	Picnic facilities all year and snack bar in picnic area (year-round, weather permitting)
Restroom Facilities	Yes
Handicapped Access	Yes
Additional Information	Wear walking shoes and dress appropriately for outdoor tour.

Conklin House
(Huntington Historical Society)

THE CONKLIN HOUSE, built c. 1750, is a farmhouse that reflects the changes that were often made in homes as they were adapted to meet the family's changing needs. Inhabited by the Conklin family until 1911, it is maintained by the Huntington Historical Society as a museum of local history and the decorative arts. There is a guided tour.

Address/Telephone	*2 High Street Huntington, NY 11743 (631) 427-7045
When to Visit	Tuesday to Friday and Sunday 1:00 p.m. to 4:00 p.m. (call first) School groups: Monday to Thursday (by appointment) 9:00 a.m. to noon
Charges/Fees	Adults—$2.50; seniors—$2.00; children under 12— $1.00; families—$5.00 max. School groups: $5.00 per child; adult chaperones— free
Suggested Grades	1–Adult
Guided Tour	Yes
Maximum Group	50, with 4 adults
Group Notice	2 weeks
Eating Facilities	None
Restroom Facilities	Yes
Handicapped Access	Limited
Additional Information	Special 90-minute program with demonstrations and hands-on crafts available for school groups. *Mailing address: 209 Main Street, Huntington, NY 11743

Heckscher Museum of Art

O N DISPLAY ARE paintings, sculptures and prints from the Heckscher Museum of Art's permanent collection of over 1,800 objects ranging from 15th-century European masterpieces to the work of contemporary American artists. The Museum presents an ambitious schedule of temporary exhibitions on an eight-to-ten-week basis. These exhibits vary from the historical to the contemporary and from showcasing international artists to explorations of the work of Long Island artists.

Address/Telephone Route 25A and Prime Avenue
Huntington, NY 11743
(631) 351-3250

Website www.heckscher.org

When to Visit Tuesday to Friday—10:00 a.m. to 5:00 p.m.
Saturday and Sunday—1:00 p.m. to 5:00 p.m.
First Friday of the month—10:00 a.m. to 8:30 p.m.

Charges/Fees $5.00 (suggested); children—$1.00

Suggested Grades All ages

Guided Tour Yes, 1 hour docent-led tours for adults.
Discovery Program for school groups:
grades K–2—1½ hours; grades 3–12—2 hours
After School Art Program for school clubs, etc.

Maximum Group 50, with adequate supervision

Group Notice 4 weeks

Eating Facilities Picnic facilities

Restroom Facilities Yes

Handicapped Access Yes

Additional Information Arrangements may be made for Discovery Program, hands-on art workshops for school groups, K through adult. For reservations and information on exhibit-related public programs call (631) 351-3250. Gallery Talks on Saturday (2:30 and 3:30 p.m.) and Sunday (1:30, 2:30, 3:30 p.m.)—no reservations required.

The Huntington Arsenal
(Town of Huntington)

THIS FULLY RESTORED building was used to store arms and ammunition during the Colonial and Revolutionary periods. Members of the Huntington Militia are present in Colonial dress, demonstrating household crafts, candle-dipping and Revolutionary-era military equipment.

Address/Telephone	*425 Park Avenue Huntington, NY 11743 (631) 351-3244
When to Visit	Sunday 1:00 p.m. to 4:00 p.m. Call if special arrangements are needed for groups.
Charges/Fees	None
Suggested Grades	K–Adult
Guided Tour	Yes, 30 minutes
Maximum Group	20
Group Notice	1 month
Eating Facilities	None
Restroom Facilities	None
Handicapped Access	No
Additional Information	*Mailing address: 228 Main Street, Huntington, NY 11743

Huntington Sewing and Trade School
(Huntington Historical Society)

THE HUNTINGTON SEWING and Trade School was built in 1905. It houses the Society's administrative offices and the Resource Center, which contains books, manuscripts, photographs and genealogies on Huntington and Long Island.

Address/Telephone	209 Main Street Huntington, NY 11743 (631) 427-7045

When to Visit	Wednesday to Friday—1:00 p.m. to 4:00 p.m. Other times by special appointment
Charges/Fees	$4.00 per person per day for use of the library for non-members
Suggested Grades	4–Adult
Guided Tour	None
Maximum Group	None
Group Notice	None
Eating Facilities	None
Restroom Facilities	Yes
Handicapped Access	No

Kissam House
(Huntington Historical Society)

THE KISSAM HOUSE was built in 1795 and is a museum of period rooms in the Colonial, Empire and Federal styles; Long Island paintings; and an outstanding collection of antique costumes. Built by Timothy Jarvis, a housewright, it boasts many fine architectural details. Adjacent to the barn is the Museum Shop, an emporium of antiques and collectibles.

Address/Telephone	*434 Park Avenue Huntington, NY 11743 (631) 427-7045
When to Visit	1:00 p.m. to 4:00 p.m. (by appointment)
Charges/Fees	Adults—$2.50; children—$1.00; seniors—$2.00
Suggested Grades	1–Adult
Guided Tour	Yes
Maximum Group	Call for information
Group Notice	Call to arrange
Eating Facilities	None
Restroom Facilities	Yes
Handicapped Access	Limited
Additional Information	*Mailing address: 209 Main Street, Huntington, NY 11743

Soldiers and Sailors Memorial Building
(Huntington Historical Society)

B UILT IN 1892, this structure was planned both as a memorial for those who gave their lives in the Civil War and as a home for the Huntington Library Association. This building, now listed on the National Register of Historic Places, provides gallery space for exhibits of Huntington Historical Society collections and houses the office of the Huntington Town Historian.

Address/Telephone	*228 Main Street (Route 25A) Huntington, NY 11743 (631) 351-3244
When to Visit	Sunday to Friday 1:00 p.m. to 4:00 p.m.
Charges/Fees	None
Suggested Grades	All ages
Guided Tour	None
Maximum Group	15
Group Notice	1 week
Eating Facilities	None
Restroom Facilities	Yes
Handicapped Access	No
Additional Information	*Mailing address: 209 Main Street, Huntington, NY 11743

Volunteers for Wildlife

V OLUNTEERS FOR WILDLIFE is a nonprofit wildlife rehabilitation and education organization, founded in 1982 to help provide rescue assistance, medical care and rehabilitation for injured and distressed wildlife on Long Island. The Volunteers for Wildlife Rehabilitation and Education Center at Caumsett State Park houses the treatment and care facility for injured and recovering wildlife. The organization provides workshops and internships to train those interested in wildlife rehabilitation. Additionally, Volunteers for Wildlife offers schools, scout groups, libraries and community organizations a selection of educational programs about Long Island wildlife.

Address/Telephone	27 Lloyd Harbor Road
	Huntington, NY 11743
	(631) 423-0982
When to Visit	By appointment
Charges/Fees	Programs at schools—$160.00 per program
	Programs at Caumsett Park Facility—$100.00 per program
Suggested Grades	Pre-K–Adult
Guided Tour	Call for schedule of program and tours
Maximum Group	30
Group Notice	2 weeks
Eating Facilities	"Brown bag"
Restroom Facilities	Yes
Handicapped Access	Yes

Empire State Carousel

THIS TRULY UNIQUE museum is an elaborate showcase for the Empire State Carousel. This full-size, hand-carved operating merry-go-round has been designed around the theme of New York State—its history, its environment, and its culture. Eighteen years in the making, this collection of colorful carousel creatures stands as tribute to the traditions of the Empire State and to the talents of the more than 1000 craftspeople who created it. In addition to the 36-foot-diameter working carousel, the museum features an active carving workshop (demonstrations on Saturdays), an ever-changing exhibit of contemporary woodcarvings, occasional woodcarving classes, and a permanent display depicting the story of merry-go-rounds and the people who made them.

> "So, bid doom and gloom farewell,
> Come ride the Empire State Carousel!"

Address/Telephone	*P.O. Box 565 Islip, NY 11751 (631) 277-6168
When to Visit	April to October Call for information
Charges/Fees	Call for information
Suggested Grades	All ages
Guided Tour	Yes, docent on duty; programs designed for school or special interest adult groups by appointment
Maximum Group	60 children with adequate supervision, or 80 adults
Group Notice	At least 1 week
Eating Facilities	Yes, nearby
Restroom Facilities	Yes
Handicapped Access	Yes
Additional Information	Gift shop specializes in unique carousel artifacts and fine craft items; a variety of publications are available. *Temporarily in storage—should be fully operational by April 2003. Please call for information.

Jamesport Vineyards

JAMESPORT VINEYARDS PRODUCES ten varieties of grapes and ten varieties of wine on its 40-acre vineyard. Visitors are given the opportunity to visit the tasting room and speak with a representative of the winery, while sampling the vintages currently available for purchasing.

Address/Telephone	Main Road Jamesport, NY 11947 Phone/Fax: (631) 722-5256 (winery)
Website	www.jamesport-vineyards.com
When to Visit	Year-round 10:00 a.m. to 5:00 p.m. Call for schedule of times and events
Charges/Fees	None
Suggested Grades	K–Adult

Guided Tour	Daily
Maximum Group	By arrangement
Group Notice	1 week
Eating Facilities	None
Restroom Facilities	Yes
Handicapped Access	Yes

BOCES Outdoor/Environmental Education Program
(Sunken Meadow State Park)

THE PRESENT AREA of Sunken Meadow State Park owes its preservation to acquisition by New York State, which gradually purchased a number of parcels of land from private persons and the Town of Smithtown. The park is comprised of 1,266 acres, which include a rocky intertidal area, sandy beach, salt marsh, climax forest vegetation and a portion of the Harbor Hill Moraine that extends along Long Island's north shore. The Learning Lab contains a variety of interesting displays concerning the natural history of Long Island. Aquaria contain numerous marine and freshwater species. The program is available to school groups.

Address/Telephone	BOCES Outdoor/Environmental Education Program
	Sunken Meadow State Park
	Parking Field #5
	Kings Park, NY 11754
	(631) 269-4343
When to Visit	Monday to Friday (school groups only)
	8:30 a.m. to 5:00 p.m.
	Summer and weekend programs by special arrangement
	Environmental Challenge Summer Program (July and August)—parents may call (631) 360-0800
Charges/Fees	BOCES shared service aid available
Suggested Grades	Pre-K–Adult

Guided Tour	By request
Maximum Group	30
Eating Facilities	Indoor/outdoor—picnic or "brown bag"
Restroom Facilities	Yes
Handicapped Access	Yes
Additional Information	Call for literature

Canoe the Nissequogue River
(Bob's Canoe Rental, Inc.)

THIS CANOE TRIP usually begins at "The Bluffs" at Kings Park where the Nissequogue empties into Long Island Sound. Timing is very critical when paddling up or down the Nissequogue since it is an estuary. A rising tide gives one the advantage when paddling from the mouth to the headwaters. Likewise, a falling tide gives the advantage when paddling downstream toward the Sound. Paddling through the reeds and marshes up the winding Nissequogue brings one to Caleb Smith State Park and the original site of three mills, one of which is still standing. The trip may begin at either end of the Nissequogue depending on the tide.

Address/Telephone	"River Mouth" *Foot of Old Dock Road Kings Park, NY 11754 (631) 269-9761 "Headwaters" *Paul T. Given Riverside Conservation Area Routes 25 and 25A (opposite the Bull) Smithtown, NY (631) 269-9761
When to Visit	Daily
Charges/Fees	$40.00—1 canoe; one-man kayak—$40.00; two-man kayak—$50.00 Call for group rates
Suggested Grades	K–Adult—adequate supervision mandatory
Guided Tour	Map of River provided

Maximum Group	144 (at 4 persons per canoe)
Group Notice	1 week
Eating Facilities	Picnic at appropriate sites along river Restaurant at mouth of river
Restroom Facilities	At Kings Park
Handicapped Access	No
Additional Information	Life jackets and paddles provided. Transportation back to car provided for one-way paddlers. Bob's Canoe Rental can also arrange trips on the Peconic River (call for information). Guided sea kayak tours. *Mailing address: P.O. Box 529, Kings Park, NY 11754

Canoe the Nissequogue River
(Nissequogue River Canoe Rentals)

THIS CANOE TRIP begins at "The Bluffs" at Kings Park where the Nissequogue empties into Long Island Sound. Timing is very critical when paddling up or down the Nissequogue since it is an estuary. A rising tide gives one the advantage when paddling from the mouth to the headwaters. Likewise, a falling tide gives the advantage when paddling downstream toward the Sound. Paddling through the reeds and marshes up the winding Nissequogue brings one to Caleb Smith State Park and the original site of three mills, one of which is still standing. The trip may begin at either end of the Nissequogue depending on the tide.

Address/Telephone	"River Mouth" *Foot of Old Dock Road Kings Park, NY 11754 (631) 979-8244
	"Headwaters" *Paul T. Given County Park Routes 25 and 25A (opposite the Bull) Smithtown, NY (631) 979-8244

Website	www.canoerentals.com
When to Visit	Daily
Charges/Fees	$40.00—1 canoe Call for group rates
Suggested Grades	K–Adult—adequate supervision mandatory
Guided Tour	Available
Maximum Group	160 (at 4 persons per canoe)
Group Notice	1 week
Eating Facilities	Picnic at appropriate sites along river Restaurant at mouth of river
Restroom Facilities	At Kings Park
Handicapped Access	No
Additional Information	Life jackets and paddles provided. Transportation back to car provided for one-way paddlers. *Mailing address: 112 Whittier Drive, Kings Park, NY 11754

Obadiah Smith House
(Smithtown Historical Society)

THIS HOUSE WAS constructed in the early 18th century with many 17th-century features. The dwelling's floor plan is similar to that of other houses built by the early descendants of Smithtown's original patentee. Of particular interest is the kitchen with its large fireplace and unusual construction. The house is backed up to a hill on its north side for protection from the winter winds. Bridges were built in order to gain access from the second floor to the hillside.

Address/Telephone	853 St. Johnland Road Kings Park, NY 11754 (631) 265-6768
Website	www.smithtownhistorical.org
When to Visit	By appointment
Charges/Fees	Donation
Suggested Grades	2–Adult

Guided Tour	Yes, 30 minutes
Maximum Group	25, with adequate supervision
Group Notice	2 weeks
Eating Facilities	None
Restroom Facilities	Yes
Handicapped Access	No
Additional Information	Programs and demonstrations by special arrangement

First Congregational Church of New Village

THIS CHURCH, WHICH now serves as a town museum, was built in 1817. The structure represents a typical old-fashioned country church. The shingled wood-frame building is a good example of period architecture and still includes some of the original windowpanes as well as some unique features.

Address/Telephone	*Middle Country Road Lake Grove, NY 11755 (631) 654-7897 Call: Mr. David A. Overton, Historian
When to Visit	Wednesday and Saturday—June to September 1:00 p.m. to 5:00 p.m. Groups by appointment
Charges/Fees	None
Suggested Grades	K–Adult
Guided Tour	Yes, 15 minutes
Maximum Group	30
Group Notice	2 weeks
Eating Facilities	None
Restroom Facilities	None
Handicapped Access	No
Additional Information	*Mailing address: 3233 Route 112, Medford, NY 11763

Lake Ronkonkoma Historical Museum
(Lake Ronkonkoma Historical Society)

T HIS MUSEUM, MAINTAINED by the Society, contains a collection of period postcards, maps and Long Island Native American artifacts. There is also an extensive collection of theatrical memorabilia from Maude Adams, who portrayed Peter Pan on Broadway. The museum offers the visitor a glimpse of the changing scenes around the lake from a small farming community to a haven for scores of people who enjoy boating, bathing and picnicking on its shores.

Address/Telephone	*328 Hawkins Avenue Lake Ronkonkoma, NY 11779 (631) 467-3152
When to Visit	Public: Saturday—10:00 a.m. to noon Groups by appointment School programs through BOCES available
Charges/Fees	Donation
Suggested Grades	Pre-K–Adult
Guided Tour	By arrangement, 1 hour
Maximum Group	25
Group Notice	2 weeks
Eating Facilities	None
Restroom Facilities	Yes
Handicapped Access	Yes, ramp (restrooms, no)
Additional Information	*Mailing address: Box 2716, Lake Ronkonkoma, NY 11779

1901 Depot Restoration and Freighthouse

V ISITORS WILL OBSERVE a complete restoration of a turn-of-the-century railroad depot and freighthouse. Inside the freighthouse is an exhibit depicting the types of trunks, barrels and specialized shipping crates used at the time, as well as the outfits and uniforms worn by railroad personnel. Visitors will also see a restored 1930s caboose. The story of "Mile-a-Minute" Murphy and exhibits of other railroad artifacts are on display.

Address/Telephone	South Broadway and South Third Street Lindenhurst, NY 11757 (631) 226-1254
When to Visit	Wednesday, Friday and Saturday July and August 2:00 p.m. to 4:00 p.m.
Charges/Fees	None
Suggested Grades	K–Adult
Guided Tour	Yes, 45 minutes, by appointment
Maximum Group	30
Group Notice	2 weeks
Eating Facilities	None
Restroom Facilities	None
Handicapped Access	No

Old Village Hall Museum

THIS MUSEUM WAS the first village-owned seat of government, containing a courtroom, the village clerk's office and a police station. Today it contains displays of articles belonging to the first permanent settlers, mementos of the Wellwood family and an exhibit tracing the evolution of Neguntatogue into Lindenhurst.

Address/Telephone	215 S. Wellwood Avenue Lindenhurst, NY 11757 (631) 957-4385 Call: Director
When to Visit	Wednesday, Friday, Saturday and first Sunday of each month—October to May Wednesday, Friday and Saturday—June to September 2:00 p.m. to 4:00 p.m. Groups by appointment

Charges/Fees	None
Suggested Grades	4–Adult
Guided Tour	Yes, 45 to 60 minutes
Maximum Group	25, with 1 adult per group of 10
Group Notice	2 weeks
Eating Facilities	None
Restroom Facilities	None
Handicapped Access	Yes

Joseph Lloyd Manor House
(Society for the Preservation of Long Island Antiquities)

L LOYD MANOR, BUILT in 1766, is a handsome structure with fine interior woodwork by Connecticut craftsmen. Located in a spectacular setting overlooking Lloyd Harbor, the grounds contain a formal garden. The house is furnished to the 1793 inventory of John Lloyd II. Lloyd Manor was the home of Jupiter Hammon, a slave who became the first published black poet in America. Interpretive exhibits provide the history and documentation for the installation.

Address/Telephone	Lloyd Lane
	Lloyd Harbor, NY 11743
	(631) 692-4664 Call: Society for the Preservation of Long Island Antiquities
Website	www.splia.org
When to Visit	Sunday
	Late May to mid-October
	1:00 p.m. to 5:00 p.m.
Charges/Fees	Adults—$3.00; children and seniors—$1.50
	Call for School Discovery Brochure and fees
Suggested Grades	2–Adult
Guided Tour	Yes, approximately 30 minutes
Maximum Group	Call for arrangements
Group Notice	2 weeks

Eating Facilities None
Restroom Facilities Yes
Handicapped Access No
Additional Information Brochure available

Target Rock National Wildlife Refuge

THIS 80-ACRE unit is one of nine refuges on Long Island (and one of over 500 throughout the United States) that provide protected habitat for migratory birds, threatened and endangered species and other wildlife. Groomed trails wind through hardwood forest, past seasonal ponds and along the rocky shore of Huntington Bay. Daffodils, rhododendrons and mountain laurel splash color throughout the trails in spring and summer. Sighting spring warblers is a must for birdwatchers!

Address/Telephone *Target Rock Road
Lloyd Neck, NY
(631) 286-0485

When to Visit Daily
½ hour before sunrise to ½ hour after sunset

Charges/Fees Vehicle—$4.00; bicyclist or pedestrian—$2.00;
large van or bus—$15.00–$25.00;
annual pass—$12.00

Suggested Grades K–Adult

Guided Tour Upon request

Maximum Group 30

Group Notice Call (631) 286-0485 one month in advance

Eating Facilities None

Restroom Facilities Yes

Handicapped Access Information kiosk, restrooms

Additional Information Location: North of Huntington; 25A to West Neck
Rd., straight onto Lloyd Harbor Rd. to Target
Rock Rd.

Note: A portion of the beach is closed to the public
April 1–September 1 due to use by threatened
and endangered species.

*Mailing address: P.O. Box 21, Shirley, NY 11967

The Animal Farm Petting Zoo

THIS IS THE perfect place to introduce children to the world of animals. See parrots, monkeys, camels, llamas, reptiles, ostrich, kangaroos and other exotic animals. There are also farm animals and their babies to pet and feed.

Address/Telephone	Wading River Road Manorville, NY 11949 (631) 878-1785
Website	www.afpz.org
When to Visit	Daily April to October 10:00 a.m. to 5:00 p.m. Weekends—10:00 a.m. to 6:00 p.m.
Charges/Fees	Adults—$12.00; children and seniors—$10.00; children under 2—free Groups call for rates
Suggested Grades	Pre-K–Adult
Guided Tour	None
Maximum Group	500
Group Notice	1 week
Eating Facilities	Yes, snack bar and picnic facilities
Restroom Facilities	Yes
Handicapped Access	Yes
Additional Information	Super Cow Musical Puppet Show, hands-on Animal Show, pony rides, turtle train and playground included with entrance fee. Safari tour train (additional fee) travels around the park.

Long Island Game Farm Children's Zoo & Family Ride Park

THE LONG ISLAND Game Farm specializes in petting areas, including: Bambiland, where you wander among the deer and hand-feed them; the Nursery, where you can bottle feed the babies; and Old MacDonald's Farmyard. It also has exotic animals including zebra, camels, bears, giraffe, ostrich, buffalo and more! It has an Antique Carousel, Safari Rail Ride, and Spinning Swings. And it has daily shows such as Alligator Feedings plus Animal Cracker Talks cage-side. From Memorial Day through Labor Day, there is also an Extreme Canine Show.

Address/Telephone	Chapman Boulevard Manorville, NY 11949 (631) 878-6644
Website	www.longislandgamefarm.com
When to Visit	Mid-April to mid-October Monday to Friday—10:00 a.m. to 5:00 p.m. Saturday and Sunday—10:00 a.m. to 6:00 p.m.
Charges/Fees	Adults—$12.95; children (2–11)—$10.95; and seniors—$7.95; children under 2—free Call for group rates or more information.
Suggested Grades	2–Adult
Guided Tour	None
Maximum Group	Unlimited, with adequate supervision
Group Notice	2 weeks, for catered picnics and birthday pavilion
Eating Facilities	Picnic facilities and refreshment stand
Restroom Facilities	Yes
Handicapped Access	Yes
Additional Information	Admission includes all rides, shows and attractions, except for pony rides. Zoomobile available.

William Floyd Estate
(Fire Island National Seashore)

TWO HUNDRED AND fifty years of history are preserved at the William Floyd Estate. Between 1718 and 1976, eight generations of Floyds managed the property and adapted it to their changing needs. The 25-room Old House, the 12 outbuildings, the graveyard and the 613 acres of forest, field and marsh illustrate the Floyd Family history in Mastic.

Address/Telephone	245 Park Drive
	Mastic Beach, NY 11951
	4 blocks north of the eastern terminus of
	Neighborhood Road in Mastic Beach
	(631) 399-2030
	Fax: (631) 399-0017
When to Visit	Open weekends only
	Memorial Day weekend through October
Charges/Fees	None
Suggested Grades	4–Adult
Guided Tour	As funding permits—please call 399-2030
Maximum Group	36, with adequate supervision
Group Notice	1 month—mandatory
Eating Facilities	Picnic tables provided
Restroom Facilities	Port-a-lavs
Handicapped Access	Yes
Additional Information	Site Operations are based on funding received each year. Please call site staff and inquire as to the status of school programs. Site staff does maintain a waiting list.

Mattituck Historical Museum and Schoolhouse
(Mattituck Historical Society)

HOUSED IN A building constructed in 1800 and expanded in 1841, this museum is furnished with antiques of the period and displays of toys and rare musical instruments. Other exhibits include century-old clothing, guns, quilts, maps and arrowheads. There is also an 1846 schoolhouse, a milk house and barn on the site.

Address/Telephone	*Main Road (Route 25) Mattituck, NY 11952 (631) 298-8089
When to Visit	Tours by appointment
Charges/Fees	Adults—$2.00; children—$1.00
Suggested Grades	3–Adult
Guided Tour	Yes, 1 to 2 hours
Maximum Group	25, with adequate supervision
Group Notice	2 weeks
Eating Facilities	None
Restroom Facilities	Yes
Handicapped Access	No
Additional Information	Summer months feature special activities on Saturday afternoons. *Mailing address: P.O. Box 766, Mattituck, NY 11952

The Long Island Philharmonic

THE LONG ISLAND Philharmonic was founded in 1979 by folk singer Harry Chapin in collaboration with Maestro Christopher Keene and several key business leaders. Currently in its 24th season, the orchestra has performed for over 2 million Long Islanders and has provided cultural and educational benefits of the highest level to the residents of Long Island. The Long Island Philharmonic offers outstanding classical concerts featuring world-class performers and Pops concerts featuring today's popular artists. The Long Island Philharmonic also offers free summer concerts, allowing the public to be entertained in the natural environment of our wonderful Long Island parks.

Address/Telephone	One Huntington Quadrangle
	Suite 2C21
	Melville, NY 11747
	(631) 293-2222, (631) 293-2223
	Fax: (631) 293-2655
Website	www.liphilharmonic.com
When to Visit	Call or write for schedule
Charges/Fees	Varies with program
Suggested Grades	K–Adult, depending on program
Guided Tour	None
Maximum Group	1,000–2,000 depending on location
Group Notice	2 weeks
Eating Facilities	None
Restroom Facilities	Yes
Handicapped Access	Yes
Additional Information	Senior/student discounts available.

The Long Island Philharmonic   BRUCE BENNETT STUDIOS

Schmitt Farm

V ISITORS WILL OBSERVE the growing of garden vegetables and some farm animals. The tour includes a wagon ride, at the conclusion of which young visitors will go to the pumpkin field, where they may choose any pumpkin they wish. There is also a farm stand on the premises where farm-fresh vegetables may be purchased. Bring your camera. Photo comedy props available.

Address/Telephone	*Exit 49 S (Walt Whitman Road) L.I. Expressway Melville, NY 11747 (631) 423-5693
When to Visit	October Monday to Friday 9:00 a.m. to 5:00 p.m. Weekends and Columbus Day—fields open to public
Charges/Fees	By arrangement
Suggested Grades	Pre-K–2
Guided Tour	None
Maximum Group	By arrangement
Group Notice	1 week
Eating Facilities	None
Restroom Facilities	Emergency only
Handicapped Access	No
Additional Information	Teachers should collect admission before visit. *Mailing address: 26 Pinelawn Rd., Melville, NY 11747

1720 William Miller House
(Miller Place–Mount Sinai Historical Society)

THE OLDEST SECTION of this colonial saltbox house dates back to 1720 and was originally built by William Miller. His descendants lived in it until 1978. Dr. Charles Millard, a Civil War surgeon, married into the Miller family and used this house for his medical practice. A display features Civil War medical instruments. Located on the property are an original Miller Place Post Office (c. 1902) and the Chereb barn (early 19th century).

Address/Telephone	*85 North Country Road Miller Place, NY 11764 (631) 476-5799
When to Visit	Sunday—1:00 p.m. to 4:00 p.m., May to September, and by appointment
Charges/Fees	None
Suggested Grades	All ages
Guided Tour	Yes, by arrangement
Maximum Group	50 (in groups of 10)
Group Notice	2 weeks
Eating Facilities	None
Restroom Facilities	None
Handicapped Access	No
Additional Information	*Mailing address: Miller Place–Mount Sinai Historical Society, P.O. Box 651, Miller Place, NY 11764

Montauk Point Lighthouse Museum
(Montauk Historical Society)

THIS FAMOUS LIGHTHOUSE marks Long Island's easternmost tip. It stands on a high bluff and was constructed by order of George Washington. Actual construction of the lighthouse began on June 7, 1796 and it was put into operation in the spring of 1797. The Montauk Historical Society maintains and preserves the lighthouse. It is still an active navigational aid and the light and foghorn are operated by the U.S. Coast Guard.

Montauk Point Lighthouse

© DICK LEWIS

Address/Telephone *2000 Montauk Highway
Montauk, NY 11954
(631) 668-2544
Fax: (631) 668-2546

Website www.montauklighthouse.com

When to Visit January 12 to May 12
Weekends only—11:00 a.m. to 4:00 p.m.
May 13 to October 13
Daily and weekends—10:30 a.m. to 4:30 p.m.
July 1 to September 1
Saturdays only—10:30 a.m. to 7:30 p.m.
Call for information and special events.

Charges/Fees Adults—$5.00; seniors—$4.50; children—$2.50
(41 inches tall to 12 years old)
Group tours: (20 or more) adults and seniors—
$3.50; children—$2.00

Suggested Grades 4–Adult
Guided Tour Yes, 30 minutes
Maximum Group 40 (minimum group: 20)
Group Notice As much notice as possible
Eating Facilities Picnic facilities and snack bar at State Park
Restroom Facilities Yes, at State Park
Handicapped Access Yes
Additional Information Gift shop on premises.
Must be at least 41 inches tall to climb the tower.
Open year-round for corporate, group and school tours with advance reservations.
*Mailing address: P.O. Box 943, Montauk, NY 11954

Spanish-American War Exhibit at Third House

THIRD HOUSE at Theodore Roosevelt County Park was built in 1806 as a cattle keeper's residence. It also served as the headquarters for Camp Wikoff where Theodore Roosevelt and his Rough Riders were quarantined in 1898 after the Spanish-American War. A Spanish-American War Exhibit displaying photos and memorabilia from the war and Camp Wikoff is open to the public Wednesdays to Sundays, Memorial Day to Columbus Day. Gift shop is available.

Address/Telephone Montauk Highway
Montauk, NY 11954
(631) 852-7878 or (631) 854-4949

When to Visit Wednesday to Sunday
Memorial Day to Columbus Day
10:00 a.m. to 5:00 p.m.
Schools and groups by special arrangement all year

Charges/Fees None
Suggested Grades 3–Adult
Guided Tour None
Maximum Group 20
Group Notice 2 weeks

Eating Facilities	Picnic grounds
Restroom Facilities	Yes
Handicapped Access	No

Viking Ferry Line

WHETHER TRAVELING OVERSEA on the *Viking Starship* or *Viking Starliner*, visits can be made to New London or Block Island. These U.S. Coast Guard-inspected and licensed vessels are modern, up-to-date passenger ships with both indoor and outdoor seating. Whale-watching and fishing trips are available in July and August.

Address/Telephone	462 West Lake Drive Montauk, NY 11954 (631) 668-5700
Website	www.vikingfleet.com
When to Visit	Call for schedule
Charges/Fees	Call for information
Suggested Grades	K–Adult, with adequate supervision
Guided Tour	None
Maximum Group	By arrangement
Group Notice	1 month
Eating Facilities	Restaurant on boat
Restroom Facilities	Yes
Handicapped Access	Limited
Additional Information	Bicycles transported for a fee

Viking Fleet/CRESLI
Whale Watch Cruises

THE VIKING FLEET offers whale watch cruises and ocean education cruises during the summer. The cruises are aboard Viking Fleet vessels out of Montauk Harbor. The education and research components of the whale

Viking Fleet/CRESLI Whale Watch Cruises

watch cruises are under the direction and leadership of The Coastal Research and Education Society of Long Island. CRESLI is a nonprofit research and educational organization specializing in marine mammals and sea turtles and whose mission is to promote and foster understanding and stewardship of coastal ecosystems through research and education.

Address/Telephone *Viking Dock
Montauk, NY 11954
(631) 668-5700

Website www.cresli.org and/or www.vikingfleet.com

When to Visit Early July through early September; Thursdays, Fridays and Saturdays

Charges/Fees Call for information

Suggested Grades 5–Adult

Maximum Group 150 (July and August)

Group Notice 7–10 days

Eating Facilities	Galley on board
Restroom Facilities	Yes
Handicapped Access	Yes
Additional Information	Warm, layered clothing advisable. Rubber-soled shoes necessary. Motion sickness medication advised. Sunglasses and sunscreen also recommended.
	*Mailing address: Coastal Research and Education Society of Long Island, Inc., Campus Box 1764, Southampton College of Long Island University, 239 Montauk Highway, Southampton, NY 11968

Mount Sinai Marine Sanctuary Nature Center

THE CENTER OFFERS a number of fresh and saltwater displays highlighting Mount Sinai Harbor's ecosystems, and a large "touch" tank holding local marine life. Also on the grounds is Brookhaven's hard clam mariculture facility where clams are produced for release into town waters.

Address/Telephone	*Harbor Beach Road Mount Sinai, NY 11766 (631) 473-8346 or (631) 451-6455
When to Visit	Daily June to September Call for current hours Groups: By special arrangement all year
Charges/Fees	None
Suggested Grades	K–Adult
Guided Tour	Yes, varies with program
Maximum Group	Unlimited
Group Notice	1 week (spring and fall tours fill early)
Eating Facilities	None
Restroom Facilities	Yes
Handicapped Access	Yes

Additional Information Town *may* impose nonresident parking fee
(Memorial Day to Labor Day)
*Mailing address: Town of Brookhaven, Nature
Center at Mt. Sinai, Division of Environmental
Protection, 3233 Route 112, Medford, NY 11763

Gemport Gallery

THIS GALLERY POSSESSES one of Long Island's largest collections of gems and minerals. On site, though not viewable by the public, jewelers work to incorporate these items into fine jewelry. These, as well as many gems and mineral specimens, are for sale to the public. New to the facility is a fluorescent mineral display which rivals that of most museums. There are also museum quality fossils—including dinosaur fossils—on display and for sale.

Address/Telephone	240 Route 25A
	Northport, NY 11768
	(631) 261-8028
When to Visit	Daily:
	10:00 a.m. to 6:00 p.m.
	Exceptions:
	Closes 8:00 p.m. Friday; opens 11:00 a.m. Sunday
	Groups by appointment
Charges/Fees	None
Suggested Grades	10–Adult
Guided Tour	Yes
Maximum Group	10
Group Notice	2 weeks
Eating Facilities	None
Restroom Facilities	Emergency only
Handicapped Access	Ramp for handicapped access
Additional Information	New Dinosaur Fossil Collection

Northport Historical Museum

THIS MUSEUM FEATURES a permanent shipbuilding exhibit as well as displays of objects and memorabilia reflecting life in the Northport area through all periods of history. The education program offers classes for elementary school children. There is a gift shop on the premises that offers appropriate collectibles and publications.

Address/Telephone	215 Main Street
	Northport, NY 11768
	(631) 757-9859
Website	www.northporthistorical.org
When to Visit	Tuesday to Sunday
	1:00 p.m. to 4:30 p.m.
	Groups by appointment
Charges/Fees	Donation
Suggested Grades	K–Adult
Guided Tour	Brochure for self-guided tour available
Maximum Group	30
Group Notice	Call for arrangement
Eating Facilities	"Brown bag"
Restroom Facilities	Yes
Handicapped Access	No

BOCES Outdoor/Environmental Education Program
(Connetquot River State Park Preserve)

THE 3,400 ACRES of Connetquot River State Park Preserve have been open to limited public access since August 1973. Prior to its acquisition by the State of New York, the property served as the site of the Southside Sportsman's Club for nearly a century. The club, described by a member as "an assembly of good-fellows," maintained the lands and waters for the protection and propagation of game birds, fish and wildlife. The Outdoor Learning Laboratory, presently located in the former main clubhouse, serves approximately 13,000 children each year and is open to school groups.

Address/Telephone	BOCES Outdoor/Environmental Education Program
	Connetquot River State Park Preserve
	Oakdale, NY 11769
	(631) 581-6016
When to Visit	Monday to Friday (school groups only)
	8:30 a.m. to 5:00 p.m.
	Summer and weekend programs by special arrangement.
Charges/Fees	BOCES shared services aid available
Suggested Grades	Pre-K–Adult
Guided Tour	By request
Maximum Group	30
Eating Facilities	Indoor/outdoor—picnic or "brown bag"
Restroom Facilities	Yes
Handicapped Access	Yes
Additional Information	Call for literature

Flax Pond Marine Laboratory

THE LABORATORY IS a research and instructional facility operated by the Marine Science Research Center of SUNY at Stony Brook. Research is conducted on the biology and ecology of fish, crustaceans, mollusks and algae. The lab is located on Flax Pond, a 147-acre tidal wetlands preserve. There is a nature trail through the marsh with explanatory material available at the laboratory.

Address/Telephone	*Crane Neck Road
	Old Field, NY
	(631) 632-8709
Website	www.msrc.sunysb.edu/flaxpond
When to Visit	Lab: Monday to Friday—8:00 a.m. to 5:00 p.m.
	Marsh: Daily—Dawn to dusk

Charges/Fees	Lab—Call for information
	Marsh—Free
Suggested Grades	Lab—3–Adult
	Marsh—All ages
Guided Tour	Lab Tour—By arrangement
	Marsh Tour—Self-guided or guided by appointment
Maximum Group	Lab—30
	Marsh—Unlimited
Group Notice	Lab—3 months
	Marsh—3 months
Eating Facilities	None
Restroom Facilities	Yes
Handicapped Access	No
Additional Information	Parking permit required: call (631) 632-8709
	*Or write: Flax Pond Manager, Marine Science Research Center, SUNY, Stony Brook, NY 11794-5000

Museum of the Oysterponds Historical Society

L OCATED IN THE picturesque village of Orient on the easternmost tip of Long Island's North Fork, the museum complex of the Oysterponds Historical Society consists of the Village House, a late-19th-century boarding house with fully furnished Victorian parlors, dining room, kitchen, boarding rooms and exhibits of glassware, Civil War material, toys and dolls; the Webb House, a late-18th-century tavern and farmhouse; and the Old Point Schoolhouse, featuring changing exhibitions of the Society's collection.

Address/Telephone	P.O. Box 70
	Village Lane
	Orient, NY 11957
	(631) 323-2480

When to Visit	Thursday, Saturday and Sunday
	2:00 p.m. to 5:00 p.m.
	July to September
	Other times by appointment
Charges/Fees	Adults—$3.00; children—$.50
Suggested Grades	2–Adult
Guided Tour	Yes, for groups by arrangement
Maximum Group	35, with at least 3 adults
Group Notice	3 weeks
Eating Facilities	Picnic area
Restroom Facilities	Yes
Handicapped Access	Yes
Additional Information	Research library open by appointment only.

Lenz Winery

GAYLE GLEASON

Lenz Winery

THE LENZ WINERY presents the visitor with 30 acres of grapes planted in the European tradition and a complex of award-winning buildings. One can see the small French oak barrels in which most of the wines are aged after fermenting in temperature-controlled stainless-steel tanks. Each season, Lenz makes a dry, Alsace-style gewürztraminer, three styles of chardonnay, a sparkling wine, a premium merlot and a cabernet sauvignon.

Address/Telephone	Main Road
	Peconic, NY 11958
	(631) 734-6010
When to Visit	Daily
	10:00 a.m. to 6:00 p.m.
Charges/Fees	Tasting fee for "reserve wines"—$2.50
Suggested Grades	4–Adult
Guided Tour	Yes, 30 minutes
Maximum Group	30
Group Notice	2 weeks
Eating Facilities	None
Restroom Facilities	Yes
Handicapped Access	No

Pindar Vineyards

A COMPLETE VINEYARD and winery experience is offered at Pindar Vineyards. This interesting and educational tour will take the visitor from the first plantings of vines through the winery operation, showing every aspect of wine creation.

Address/Telephone	P.O. Box 332
	Main Road
	Peconic, NY 11958
	(631) 734-6200
Website	www.pindar.net

When to Visit	Daily
	11:00 a.m. to 6:00 p.m.
Charges/Fees	None—except for group tours (Call ahead)
Suggested Grades	4–Adult
Guided Tour	Yes, by arrangement
Maximum Group	100
Group Notice	1 month
Eating Facilities	None
Restroom Facilities	Yes
Handicapped Access	Yes

Mather House Museum
(Port Jefferson Historical Society)

THIS MUSEUM IS located in the homestead of the Mathers, a prominent shipbuilding family. The museum features a number of permanent exhibits, one of which highlights the harbor's early shipbuilding industry with displays of shipbuilding tools, models and photographs of early harbor activities. The museum complex includes a marine barn, toolshed, craft house, replicas of a country store, barber shop and butcher, and herb and perennial gardens, and the Spinney clock collection.

Address/Telephone	*115 Prospect Street
	Port Jefferson, NY 11777
	(631) 473-2665 or (631) 928-6287 (Curator)
When to Visit	1:00 p.m. to 4:00 p.m.
	Saturday and Sunday—May 23 to June, and
	September 1 to Labor Day
	Tuesday, Wednesday, Saturday and Sunday—
	July and August
Charges/Fees	$2.00
Suggested Grades	K–Adult
Guided Tour	Yes—45 minutes
Maximum Group	35

Group Notice	2 weeks minimum
Eating Facilities	None
Restroom Facilities	Yes
Handicapped Access	No
Additional Information	*Mailing address: Box 586, Port Jefferson, NY 11777

Theatre Three

T HEATRE THREE IS Suffolk's only year-round professional theater. Theatre Three presents seven Main Stage and three Second Stage productions each year, as well as nine fully staged, in-house children's musicals and five topical touring shows. It also offers drama classes for young people and adults.

Address/Telephone	*412 Main Street Port Jefferson, NY 11777 Public: (631) 928-9100 Group Sales: (631) 928-1130 Business Office: (631) 928-9202 Touring information only: call (631) 928-2624
When to Visit	Call for schedule
Charges/Fees	Call for information
Suggested Grades	Pre-K–Adult, depending on production
Guided Tour	None
Maximum Group	400
Group Notice	1 month
Eating Facilities	None
Restroom Facilities	Yes
Handicapped Access	No
Additional Information	Call for further information on touring theater programs. *Mailing address: P.O. Box 512, Port Jefferson, NY 11777

Kids for Kids Productions, Inc.

THIS ORGANIZATION, WHICH is designed to train young people in all aspects of the theater, presents professional performances to the public at local schools. Workshop sessions emphasizing skill development in drama, voice, movement and dance are also available.

Address/Telephone	St. Paul's Lutheran Church
	309 Patchogue Road (Route 112)
	Port Jefferson Station, NY 11776
	(631) 476-2169
	Fax: (631) 474-1607
	Email: k4kpro@aol.com
Website	www.geocities.com/k4kpro/index.html
When to Visit	Call or write for schedule
Charges/Fees	Adults—$10.00; children (K–12)—$8.00;
	senior citizens and bonafide groups—$6.00
Suggested Grades	Pre-K–Adult
Guided Tour	By arrangement
Group Notice	2 to 4 weeks
Eating Facilities	None
Restroom Facilities	Yes
Handicapped Access	Yes
Additional Information	Workshops on theater skills for youngsters age 4–10.

Old School House Museum

THIS SCHOOLHOUSE WAS built in 1822, cost $350 to build and was said at the time to be "the largest and best in Suffolk County." Its original location was at the edge of Quogue Street, somewhat west of its present site. The building was used as a schoolhouse and community meeting-place from 1822 until 1893. A collection of relics of Quogue's early history, farm and household implements, old letters, maps, collections of photographs and old toys are displayed.

Address/Telephone	*90 Quogue Street Quogue, NY 11959 (631) 653-4224
When to Visit	July 1 to Labor Day Wednesday and Friday—3:00 p.m. to 5:00 p.m. Saturday—10:00 a.m. to noon
Charges/Fees	None
Suggested Grades	5–Adult
Guided Tour	None
Maximum Group	10
Group Notice	2 weeks
Eating Facilities	None
Restroom Facilities	At library for emergencies
Handicapped Access	No
Additional Information	*Mailing address: P.O. Box 1207, Quogue, NY 11959

Quogue Wildlife Refuge

THIS REFUGE CONTAINS 300 acres of varied natural and managed habitats encompassing the headwaters of Quantuck Creek in Quogue. Nature trails (which are wheelchair-accessible) reveal a wide cross section of ecological habitats, including ponds, swamp, freshwater bog, estuary and pine barrens. Located at the entrance to the refuge is a Distressed Wildlife Complex housing incapacitated birds and animals. These animals are permanently disabled and require human intervention to survive.

Address/Telephone	Old Main Road and Old Country Road Quogue, NY 11959 (631) 653-4771
Website	www.quoguerefuge.com
When to Visit	Daily Sunrise to sunset
Charges/Fees	None for individuals and families—only for groups wanting a guide, then by appointment

Suggested Grades K–Adult

Guided Tour Yes, call for information

Group Notice Self-guided: 1 week
Guided group tours: Call for appointment
and fees

Eating Facilities None

Restroom Facilities Yes

Handicapped Access Most of refuge is wheelchair-accessible

Additional Information Nature Center with nature library and natural
history exhibits open Tuesdays and Thursdays,
1:00 p.m. to 4:00 p.m., and Saturdays and Sundays, 11:00 a.m. to 4:00 p.m.
Ice Harvesting Museum with historical display of
ice-cutting tools and methods.

Canoe the Peconic River
(Peconic Paddler)

A CANOE TRIP along the Peconic River begins where the river is a very
narrow stream at Connecticut Avenue in Calverton. When you
approach the final destination near the traffic circle in the Village of Riverhead, you will have traveled through cranberry bogs and marshland and
over dams, and portaged three times. This river, which eventually empties
into Flanders Bay, is primarily fed through the underground aquifer.

Address/Telephone 89 Peconic Avenue
Riverhead, NY 11901
(631) 727-9895

Website www.peconicpaddler.com

Peconic Paddler

When to Visit	Monday to Friday—8:00 a.m., 10:00 a.m. and noon
	Saturday and Sunday—(every half-hour) 8:00 a.m. to noon
	Reservations recommended
Charges/Fees	$45.00—1 canoe
Suggested Grades	K–Adult—adequate supervision mandatory
Guided Tour	Map and instructions provided
Maximum Group	100
Group Notice	2 weeks
Eating Facilities	Picnic at appropriate sites along river. Restaurants at portage and Riverhead.
Restroom Facilities	Yes, at portage and Riverhead
Handicapped Access	No
Additional Information	Life jackets and paddles provided

Hallockville Museum Farm

L OCATED ON EASTERN Long Island's scenic North Fork, the Hallockville Museum Farm is an eight-acre complex of original 18th- and 19th-century farm buildings, including the c. 1765 Hallock Homestead, a large barn, a shoemaker's shop, workshop, smokehouse and outhouse. Occupied for nearly 200 years by five generations of the Hallock family, the site is one of the oldest intact farms on Long Island and is listed on the National Register of Historic Places. Open year-round, we offer tours, permanent and temporary exhibits, craft demonstrations, festivals, school programs, workshops, lectures and much more!

Address/Telephone	6038 Sound Avenue Riverhead, NY 11901 (631) 298-5292
When to Visit	Wednesday to Saturday 11:00 a.m. to 4:00 p.m.
Charges/Fees	Adults—$5.00; seniors—$4.00; children (6–16)—$2.00; children under 6—free
Suggested Grades	K–Adult
Guided Tour	Orientation—followed by guided tour
Maximum Group	100
Group Notice	2 weeks; call for group rates.
Eating Facilities	Yes, picnic facilities
Restroom Facilities	Yes, handicapped-accessible
Handicapped Access	Some buildings

Long Island Horticultural Research and Extension Center (Cornell University)

T HE LONG ISLAND Horticultural Research and Extension Center is a site where applied agricultural research is conducted on vegetables, grapes, nursery and greenhouse plants and turfgrass. Plant problems such as diseases, weeds, and insects are investigated as part of the overall program.

Address/Telephone	3059 Sound Avenue Riverhead, NY 11901 (631) 727-3595
When to Visit	Tours on a scheduled basis only. Groups wishing to visit should write or phone Coordinator's Office.
Charges/Fees	None
Suggested Grades	8–Adult
Guided Tour	Yes, 1 hour in length, including an informal talk regarding experiments in progress at the time
Maximum Group	30
Group Notice	2 weeks
Eating Facilities	None
Restroom Facilities	Emergency only
Handicapped Access	No

Riverhead Foundation for Marine Research and Preservation (Aquarium Preview Center)

THE FOUNDATION'S AQUARIUM Preview Center features 13 fresh and salt-water tanks depicting Long Island's aquatic environments, rehabilitating sea turtles, a 22-foot marine touch tank and, when available, the seal house exhibits female Harbor Seals being rehabilitated. We also offer group tours, slide presentations and lectures. Gift shop.

Address/Telephone	431 East Main Street Riverhead, NY 11901 (631) 369-9840
Website	www.riverheadfoundation.org
When to Visit	Daily in summer—9:00 a.m. to 5:00 p.m. Call for winter hours Group tours/lectures available all year by appointment

Charges/Fees	Adults—$4.00; children—$2.00
	Tours—call for fees
Suggested Grades	All ages
Guided Tour	Yes, by appointment
Maximum Group	30
Group Notice	1 week
Eating Facilities	Picnic tables
Restroom Facilities	Yes
Handicapped Access	Yes
Additional Information	Adopt a seal, sea turtle or whale program

Splish Splash
(Long Island's Water Park)

S PLISH SPLASH was voted one of America's Top 5 Water Parks by the Travel Channel. This 96-acre facility features a variety of water activities, including 18 water slides, a wave pool, a 1,300-foot-long lazy river, diving show and bird show. "New for 2002" is The Hollywood Stunt Rider, a totally in the dark family raft ride with an interactive queue line. So much fun, so close to home!

Address/Telephone	2549 Splish Splash Drive
	P.O. Box 1090
	Riverhead, NY 11901
	(631) 727-3600
Website	www.splishsplashlongisland.com
When to Visit	Weekends and holidays—Memorial Day weekend to mid-June
	Daily—mid-June until first week in September
Charges/Fees	Call for information
Suggested Grades	All ages
Guided Tour	Yes

Maximum Group None
Group Notice Yes, at least 48 hours in advance with reservations
Eating Facilities Restaurant featuring burgers, hot dogs,
deli sandwiches, pizza, churros, pretzels,
ice cream and more
Restroom Facilities Yes
Handicapped Access Limited

Suffolk County Courts

THIS TRIP OFFERS young people a special lecture on the criminal justice system and court systems of New York State and Suffolk County. A visit to an operating courtroom is part of the tour. Depending on the calendar of courtroom activities for the day, students may witness courtroom procedures such as jury selection and jury trials.

Address/Telephone Chief Thomas F. Lorito
Chief Court Officer
Criminal Courts Building
Center Drive
Riverhead, NY 11901
(631) 852-1712

When to Visit Criminal Courts Building—Riverhead
Tours on Tuesday and Wednesday
By appointment only
Cohalan Court Complex—Islip
Tours on Monday, Wednesday and Thursday
By appointment only

Charges/Fees None
Suggested Grades 6–Adult
Guided Tour Yes, 10:00 a.m. to 12:30 p.m.
Maximum Group 25

Group Notice As much as possible. Schedule fills up months in
advance.

Eating Facilities None

Restroom Facilities Yes

Handicapped Access Yes

Additional Information For further community outreach programs, please
contact Patricia Herlihy at (631) 853-7626.

Suffolk County Historical Society

T HE SUFFOLK COUNTY Historical Society's collections, exhibitions and
programs concentrate on the history of Suffolk County and its people.
The combined resources of the museum, research library and archives and
education programs uniquely enable the Society to bring Suffolk County
history to life for visitors of all ages. The Society offers a variety of
programs for visiting school groups along with programs for adults and
children throughout the year.

Address/Telephone 300 West Main Street (Route 25)
Riverhead, NY 11901
(631) 727-2881

When to Visit Museum: Tuesday to Saturday
12:30 p.m. to 4:30 p.m.
Library: Wednesday, Thursday and Saturday
12:30 p.m. to 4:30 p.m.
Groups and morning visits by appointment

Charges/Fees Museum: Free admission, donations accepted.
Library: $2.00 per day for non-member library
users.

Suggested Grades K–Adult

Guided Tour Yes, 1 hour (by appointment)

Maximum Group 30

Group Notice 2 weeks

Eating Facilities None
Restroom Facilities Yes
Handicapped Access No

Suffolk County Legislature

V ISITORS WILL HAVE the opportunity to observe the 18-member Suffolk County Legislature debate, formulate and pass or defeat proposed laws and spending bills. The Legislature also holds many legal and public hearings as well as public presentations. Depending on the business of the day, opportunities may present themselves to visit and discuss governmental problems with local representatives and other County officials.

Address/Telephone Riverhead County Center
Riverhead, NY 11901
(631) 852-1700

William H. Rogers Legislature Building
Hauppauge County Center
725 Veterans' Memorial Highway
Smithtown, NY 11787
(631) 853-4070

When to Visit Meetings alternate between Hauppauge and Riverhead.
Call for further information.

Charges/Fees None

Suggested Grades 7–Adult

Guided Tour Yes, tour of County facilities by arrangement

Maximum Group 30

Group Notice 1 week

Eating Facilities None

Restroom Facilities Yes

Handicapped Access Yes

Additional Information Call to arrange for seminars and special programs.
Also call for scheduled "mock legislature" sessions that students take part in (duration—40 minutes).

Suffolk County Maximum Security Facility

V̶ISITS TO THE Suffolk County Maximum Security Facility are offered under the Y.E.S. (Youth Enlightenment Seminar) Program. The program is designed to serve as a learning experience for Criminal Justice classes from Suffolk County. The program utilizes the negative realities of incarceration to serve as a deterrent for adolescents who might be prone to criminal behavior in the future, and offers information on law enforcement careers.

Address/Telephone	100 Center Drive Riverhead, NY 11901 (631) 852-3763
When to Visit	By appointment
Charges/Fees	None
Suggested Grades	7–Adult
Guided Tour	Yes, 2½ hours
Maximum Group	40
Group Notice	Make reservations well in advance
Eating Facilities	None
Restroom Facilities	Yes
Handicapped Access	Yes
Additional Information	In order to participate in this program, contact Community Relations. The Sheriff's Office also provides presentations suitable for classrooms and school assemblies, and safety programs for grades K–12.

Custom House

I̶N 1789, SAG HARBOR became a United States Port of Entry. This building was the first Custom House in New York State and the first post office on Long Island. The furnishings illustrate the sophisticated Eastern lifestyle of the period, including many Dering and other Sag Harbor family pieces and pictures.

Address/Telephone	Garden Street
	Sag Harbor, NY 11963
	(631) 692-4664 Call: Society for the Preservation of Long Island Antiquities
Website	www.splia.org
When to Visit	Daily—July to August
	Weekends only—June and September
	10:00 a.m. to 5:00 p.m.
	Groups by appointment
Charges/Fees	Adults—$3.00; children—$1.50; children under 6—free
	Call for group rates
Suggested Grades	2–Adult
Guided Tour	Yes, 20–30 minutes
Maximum Group	By arrangement
Group Notice	2 weeks
Eating Facilities	None
Restroom Facilities	Yes
Handicapped Access	No
Additional Information	Do not touch antiques.

Custom House

Elizabeth A. Morton
National Wildlife Refuge

THIS 187-ACRE PENINSULA is one of nine refuges on Long Island (and one of over 500 throughout the United States) that provide protected habitat for migratory birds, threatened and endangered species and other wildlife. A ¾-mile trail leads to the sandy beach and steep bluffs that fringe the peninsula. A ½-mile loop trail winds through the forested inland portion of the Refuge.

Address/Telephone *Noyack Road
Sag Harbor, NY 11963
(631) 286-0485

When to Visit Daily
½ hour before sunrise to ½ hour after sunset

Charges/Fees Vehicle—$4.00; bicyclist or pedestrian—$2.00;
large van or bus—$15.00–$25.00;
annual pass—$12.00

Suggested Grades K–Adult

Guided Tour Upon request

Maximum Group 30

Group Notice Call (631) 286-0485 one month in advance

Eating Facilities None

Restroom Facilities Yes

Handicapped Access Information Kiosk, restrooms

Additional Information Location: Three miles west of Sag Harbor on
Noyack Road.
Note: A portion of the beach is closed to the public
April 1–September 1 due to use by threatened
and endangered species.
*Mailing address: P.O. Box 21, Shirley, NY 11967

Sag Harbor Whaling and
Historical Museum

As YOU ENTER this museum you will pass through the bones of a right whale. These genuine jawbones were brought home by a Sag Harbor whaler and have been on display for over 100 years. The museum covers the history of whaling on Long Island over the last century. It displays logs recording the voyages of ships, whaling equipment, scrimshaw, period furniture and ship models.

Address/Telephone	*200 Main Street
	Sag Harbor, NY 11963
	(631) 725-0770 or (631) 725-1094
Website	www.sagharborwhalingmuseum.org
When to Visit	May to October 1
	Monday to Saturday—10:00 a.m. to 5:00 p.m.
	Sunday—1:00 p.m. to 5:00 p.m.
Charges/Fees	Adults—$3.00; children (6–13)—$1.00; seniors—
	$2.00
Suggested Grades	3–Adult—call for group rates
Guided Tour	By appointment
Maximum Group	50
Group Notice	3 weeks
Eating Facilities	Picnic facilities
Restroom Facilities	Yes
Handicapped Access	Handicap ramp available
Additional Information	Historian available at museum.
	*Mailing address: Box 1327, Sag Harbor, NY 11963

The Brewster House

IN A PROGRAM entitled "A Day in the Life of a Colonial Child," students become history detectives as they step back in time and relive the daily life of a colonial family. Through visual presentation of architecture, decorative arts, household tools and lifestyle, students are able to comprehend historical and economic concepts. Interactive activities allow students to experience 18th-century tasks and games. Another program focuses on the Revolutionary War—the importance of George Washington's Spy Ring and the dangers involved in this clandestine operation. Students trace the creation and coordination of the spy operation and code messages as they locate the spies' six landing spots. The code of silence, secret security measures and the techniques of key American and British spies are discussed. Students discover how messages were decoded utilizing letter masking and invisible ink.

Decorated in period furniture and transformed over the centuries from a one-room cottage to the present salt box structure, the Brewster House was home to six generations of Brewsters. Reverend Nathaniel Brewster, the homestead's first owner, was the Setauket settlement's first ordained minister. Another family member, Caleb Brewster, was a member of George Washington's Spy Ring during the Revolutionary War.

Address/Telephone	Route 25A
	Setauket, NY 11733
	For reservations:
	The Ward Melville Heritage Organization
	P.O. Box 572
	Stony Brook, NY 11790
	(631) 751-2244
Website	www.wardmelvilleheritage.org
When to Visit	By appointment
Charges/Fees	$5.00 per person (adults included/teacher exempt)
	$60.00 minimum
Suggested Grades	Can be tailored to appropriate grade levels
Guided Tour	Yes
Maximum Group	30
Group Notice	Call for information
Eating Facilities	Yes, nearby
Restroom Facilities	Yes
Handicapped Access	Limited
Additional Information	The house is available for educational programs only.

The Thompson House
(Society for the Preservation of Long Island Antiquities)

BUILT IN 1700, the Thompson House offers a vivid portrait of 18th-century family life and customs on Long Island. Unusually large with superb early architectural details, it houses one of the finest collections of early Long Island furniture. A Colonial herb garden is maintained on the grounds.

Address/Telephone 93 North Country Road
Setauket, NY 11733
(631) 692-4664 Call: Society for the Preservation
of Long Island Antiquities

Website www.splia.org

When to Visit Friday, Saturday and Sunday
late May to mid-October
1:00 p.m. to 5:00 p.m.

Charges/Fees Adults—$3.00; children and seniors—$1.50
Call for school discovery brochure and fees

Suggested Grades 2–Adult

Guided Tour Yes, 45 minutes

Maximum Group By arrangement

Group Notice 2 weeks

Eating Facilities None

Restroom Facilities None

Handicapped Access No

Additional Information Special events held on the grounds annually.

Havens House
(Shelter Island Historical Society)

B UILT C. 1743 with a mid-19th-century addition, the Havens House served
as a residence, post office and general store. Part of the original construction has been left exposed for inspection. Textiles and furnishings span the occupancy of the Havens family (mid-18th to early 19th centuries).

Address/Telephone 16 South Ferry Road (Route 114)
Shelter Island, NY 11964
(631) 749-0025
Email: sihissoc@hamptons.com

When to Visit Friday, Saturday and Sunday—11:00 a.m. to
3:00 p.m. (May 15–September 15)
Other hours by appointment

Charges/Fees Adults—$2.00; children—$1.00

Suggested Grades 4–Adult

Guided Tour Call for information

Maximum Group	30
Group Notice	2 weeks
Eating Facilities	None
Restroom Facilities	No
Handicapped Access	No
Additional Information	The house is situated on the main road between North and South Ferry. Manhanset Chapel Museum is a half-mile north.

The Mashomack Preserve
(The Nature Conservancy)

THE MASHOMACK PRESERVE consists of 2,039 acres of oak woodlands, marshes, freshwater ponds and interlacing tidal creeks, edged in white by 10 miles of coastline. This green peninsula still hosts ibis and hummingbirds, muskrats and foxes, harbor seals and terrapins. Together with nearby Gardiners Island, the Mashomack area supports one of the East Coast's largest concentrations of nesting osprey. Its woods and wetland harbor rare plants, native orchids, lichens and a variety of ferns. There is a gift shop (open seasonally and on weekends) that also houses small displays.

Address/Telephone	*79 South Ferry Road Shelter Island, NY 11964 (631) 749-1001
Website	www.nature.org
When to Visit	Wednesday to Monday 9:00 a.m. to 5:00 p.m. Open 7 days a week (July and August)
Charges/Fees	Adults—$2.00; children—$1.00
Suggested Grades	K–Adult
Guided Tour	Yes, by arrangement. 1 to 2½ hours for groups of 10 or more
Maximum Group	30
Group Notice	2 weeks

Eating Facilities	None
Restroom Facilities	Yes
Handicapped Access	Yes
Additional Information	*Mailing address: P.O. Box 850, Shelter Island, NY 11964

Wertheim National Wildlife Refuge

THIS 2,550-ACRE UNIT is one of nine refuges on Long Island (and one of over 500 throughout the United States) that provide protected habitat for migratory birds, threatened and endangered species and other wildlife. The Refuge is bisected by the Carmans River, a state-designated Wild and Scenic River. A trail (consisting of a 1.5-mile loop and a 3-mile loop), meanders through forested upland areas and offers views of the Carmans River and associated wetlands. Guided programs by appointment. Call for event schedule.

Address/Telephone	*Smith Road Shirley, NY 11967 (631) 286-0485
When to Visit	Daily 8:00 a.m. to 4:30 p.m. (except federal holidays)
Charges/Fees	None
Suggested Grades	K–Adult
Guided Tour	Upon request
Maximum Group	30
Group Notice	Call (631) 286-0485 one month in advance
Eating Facilities	None
Restroom Facilities	Yes
Handicapped Access	Information Kiosk, Refuge Office, restrooms, ½-mile portion of trail (to open Summer 2002)
Additional Information	Location: On Smith Road, ½-mile west of the William Floyd Parkway and ⅓-mile south of Route 80 (Montauk Highway). Note: Canoe access to the Carmans River nearby. *Mailing address: P.O. Box 21, Shirley, NY 11967

BOCES Outdoor/Environmental Education Program
(Caleb Smith State Park Preserve)

T HE 543-ACRE CALEB Smith State Park Preserve is one of the last tracts of undeveloped land on Long Island and is a refuge for organisms displaced by the rapid and extensive growth of suburbia. Botanically, the park maintains a high diversity of over 200 plant species composing several plant communities. The Program is held in a reconstructed 120-year-old barn and stable and is available to school classes.

Address/Telephone	BOCES Outdoor/Environmental Education Program Caleb Smith State Park 810 Meadow Road Smithtown, NY 11787 (631) 360-3652
When to Visit	Monday to Friday (school groups only) 8:30 a.m. to 5:00 p.m. Summer and weekend programs by special arrangement
Charges/Fees	BOCES shared service aid available
Suggested Grades	Pre-K–Adult
Guided Tour	By request
Maximum Group	30
Eating Facilities	Indoor-outdoor—picnic or "brown bag"
Restroom Facilities	Yes
Handicapped Access	Yes
Additional Information	Call for literature

Caleb Smith House
(Smithtown Historical Society)

T HE CALEB SMITH House, presently located on Smithtown's Village Green, was originally built in 1819 and located on Jericho Turnpike in Commack. The House now serves as a headquarters for the Smithtown

Historical Society and a repository for documents and books relating to the history of Smithtown. Artifacts of local interest, including pieces of furniture once owned by the Smith and Blydenburgh families, are on display.

Address/Telephone 5 North Country Road
Smithtown, NY 11787
(631) 265-6768

Website www.smithtownhistorical.org

When to Visit Monday to Friday (all year)—9:00 a.m. to 4:00 p.m.
Saturday—by appointment
Groups by appointment only

Charges/Fees Donation

Suggested Grades 2–Adult

Guided Tour Yes, 15 minutes

Maximum Group 30, with adequate supervision

Group Notice 2 weeks

Caleb Smith House

Eating Facilities	None
Restroom Facilities	Yes
Handicapped Access	No

Epnetus Smith Tavern
(Smithtown Historical Society)

T HE WEST WING of this building dates back to 1690. The Inn was added c. 1750. Moved three times from its original site, the building accommodated British troops during the Revolution and, in more recent times, the Smithtown Library.

Address/Telephone	211 E. Middle Country Road Smithtown, NY 11787 (631) 265-6768
Website	www.smithtownhistorical.org
When to Visit	Schools and groups only, by appointment
Charges/Fees	$6.00 per child
Suggested Grades	4–8
Guided Tour	Program only
Maximum Group	30
Group Notice	2 weeks
Eating Facilities	"Brown bag"
Restroom Facilities	Yes
Handicapped Access	Yes
Additional Information	Special school program on the role of the tavern in life in early America, by arrangement

Franklin O. Arthur Farm
(Smithtown Historical Society)

P RESENTLY MANAGED BY the Smithtown Historical Society, the Franklin O. Arthur House was built sometime between 1730 and 1750. With hopes of opening the facility as a farm museum in the not too distant future, the Society at present uses the house as a learning center for schools and youth groups.

Address/Telephone	245 E. Middle Country Road Smithtown, NY 11787 (631) 265-6768
Website	www.smithtownhistorical.org
When to Visit	By appointment
Charges/Fees	School program—$6.00 per child
Suggested Grades	4–8
Guided Tour	Program only
Maximum Group	30
Group Notice	Book early in September
Eating Facilities	"Brown bag"
Restroom Facilities	Yes
Handicapped Access	Yes
Additional Information	Hands-on Colonial craft program, emphasizing fiber preparation, dyeing, spinning and weaving

Judge J. Lawrence Smith Homestead
(Smithtown Historical Society)

B UILT DURING THE 18th century and enlarged c. 1835, the Homestead was the residence and law office of Judge Lawrence Smith. It is presently used as a learning center focused on the 19th century.

Address/Telephone	205 Middle Country Road
	Smithtown, NY 11787
	(631) 265-6768
Website	www.smithtownhistorical.org
When to Visit	Schools and groups by appointment
Charges/Fees	School program—$6.00 per child
Suggested Grades	4–8
Guided Tour	School program only
Maximum Group	30
Group Notice	2 weeks
Eating Facilities	"Brown bag"
Restroom Facilities	Yes
Handicapped Access	Yes
Additional Information	Special school program on the 19th century

Richard H. Handley
Long Island History Room
(Smithtown Library)

THE HANDLEY LONG ISLAND History Room is the repository for an important collection of books, pamphlets, newspapers, photographs, manuscripts and maps relating to Long Island and the Town of Smithtown. Included are genealogies of many Long Island families.

Address/Telephone	One North Country Road
	Smithtown, NY 11787
	(631) 265-2072
When to Visit	Monday to Thursday—10:00 a.m. to 9:00 p.m.
	Friday—10:00 a.m. to 6:00 p.m.
	Saturday—10:00 a.m. to 5:00 p.m.
	Sunday—1:00 p.m. to 5:00 p.m.
	(except Summer)
	School groups by appointment
Charges/Fees	None

Suggested Grades 4–Adult (children under grade 9 should be
supervised by adults)

Guided Tour Workshops by arrangement

Maximum Group 12

Group Notice 1 week

Eating Facilities None

Restroom Facilities Yes

Handicapped Access Yes

Additional Information Materials are for use in the library only.

Captain Albert Rogers Mansion
(Southampton Historical Museum)

BUILT IN 1843 by a whaling captain, the Rogers Mansion is the head-quarters of the Southampton Historical Museum. With period rooms, changing exhibition galleries and a large collection of decorative arts including dolls and toys, this museum represents the 19th and early 20th centuries of Southampton's town history. On the grounds is a collection of small shops and barns (moved here) that help recreate a vision of the post-Civil War period, including a paint and wallpaper shop, one-room school-house, blacksmith shop, carpenter shop, general store and others. The Nugent Carriage Barn houses an interesting gathering of farming and whaling tools.

Address/Telephone 17 Meeting House Lane
P.O. Box 303
Southampton, NY 11969
(631) 283-2494
Email: hismusdir@hamptons.com

Website www.southamptonhistoricalmuseum.com

When to Visit May through December
Tuesday to Saturday—11:00 a.m. to 5:00 p.m.
Sunday—1:00 p.m. to 5:00 p.m.
January through April
Tuesday to Saturday—11:00 a.m. to 5:00 p.m.

Charges/Fees	Adults—$3.00; seniors—$2.00; students—$1.00
Suggested Grades	K–Adult
Guided Tour	Orientation with self-guided tour
Maximum Group	50
Group Notice	By reservation
Eating Facilities	Picnic area
Restroom Facilities	Yes
Handicapped Access	First floors only

Conscience Point Historic Site and Nature Walk
(Southampton Historical Museum)

THIS IS THE sight of the landing of the first Pilgrim English immigrants from Lynn, Massachusetts, in 1640. This quiet and lovely area offers a beautiful view of the Peconic Bay and the nature trail leads through a rich variety of native shore plants. The Colonists most likely camped here, and with the help of Shinnecock guides, the English went to Old Town where they settled until about 1648, when Main Street was laid out.

Address/Telephone	North Sea Road
	North Sea Harbor
	Southampton, NY 11968
	(631) 283-2494
	Email: hismusdir@hamptons.com
Website	www.southamptonhistoricalmuseum.com
When to Visit	Open daily
Charges/Fees	Free
Suggested Grades	K–Adult
Guided Tour	None
Eating Facilities	Picnic by the bay
Restroom Facilities	No
Handicapped Access	No

The Parrish Art Museum

The Parrish Art Museum

ESTABLISHED IN 1898, this museum provides numerous cultural programs for eastern Suffolk communities. Included are changing exhibitions of 19th and 20th century American art, lectures, adult and children's workshops, jazz concerts, classical music concerts and children's theater. The permanent collection includes 19th-century etchings and American art, with extensive holdings of works by William Merritt Chase and Fairfield Porter. The museum also includes an arboretum, sculpture garden and museum shop.

Address/Telephone 25 Job's Lane
Southampton, NY 11968
(631) 283-2118

When to Visit Monday, Thursday, Friday, Saturday
11:00 a.m. to 5:00 p.m.
Exception: Sunday—1:00 p.m. to 5:00 p.m.
Summer hours: Open daily—June 1 to September 15

Charges/Fees	$5.00 suggested donation; seniors and students—$2.00
Suggested Grades	Varies with program, call in advance
Guided Tour	Yes
Maximum Group	35
Group Notice	1 week
Eating Facilities	None
Restroom Facilities	Yes
Handicapped Access	Wheelchair access available
Additional Information	Museum shop

Pelletreau Goldsmith Shop
(Southampton Historical Museum)

A RARE SURVIVOR of 18th-century commercial life, this tiny gambrel-roofed shop has been restored to the working period of Southampton's famous craftsman, Elias Pelletreau, who created masterpieces of Colonial silver here between 1750 and 1810. From his ancient workbench filled with tools to his forge, you can experience the life of an 18th-century worker, complete with examples of his silver.

Address/Telephone	74 Main Street
	Southampton, NY 11968
	(631) 283-2494
	Email: hismusdir@hamptons.com
Website	www.southamptonhistoricalmuseum.com
When to Visit	Friday to Sunday
	2nd week of July to Columbus Day weekend
	11:00 a.m. to 5:00 p.m. (Friday and Saturday)
	1:00 p.m. to 5:00 p.m. (Sunday)
Charges/Fees	Free
Suggested Grades	K–Adult
Guided Tour	Yes

Maximum Group	10
Group Notice	2 weeks
Eating Facilities	None
Restroom Facilities	No
Handicapped Access	No

Southampton Hospital

THIS 164-BED NONPROFIT medical center offers a full continuum of inpatient and outpatient diagnostic, therapeutic and rehabilitative services. It is Eastern Long Island's largest hospital and the South Fork's only major medical facility. In addition to the main campus located in Southampton Village, the hospital has several satellite facilities located in East Hampton, Greenport, Hampton Bays, Quogue and Westhampton Beach. Staffed by more than 230 physicians, dentists and allied health professionals representing at least 39 medical and surgical practice areas, Southampton Hospital stands ready to serve the Eastern Long Island community.

Address/Telephone	240 Meeting House Lane
	Southampton, NY 11968
	(631) 726-8700 (Public Affairs)
When to Visit	Monday to Friday—9:00 a.m. to 4:00 p.m.
	By appointment only
Charges/Fees	None
Suggested Grades	7–Adult
Guided Tour	Yes
Maximum Group	12
Group Notice	3 weeks
Eating Facilities	Cafeteria and coffee shop
Restroom Facilities	Yes
Handicapped Access	Yes

Thomas Halsey House
(Southampton Historical Museum)

THE THOMAS HALSEY HOUSE is one of the oldest houses in New York State. Built on the site of his father's house (1648), Thomas completed his home about 1678. The house is filled with beautiful 17th- and 18th-century antiques and adorned with early textiles and rare ceramics, which create the sense that it is still inhabited by the family. The beautiful grounds are complete with an 18th-century herb garden, a spectacular perennial border and an old orchard.

Address/Telephone	249 South Main Street
	Southampton, NY 11968
	(631) 283-2494
	Email: hismusdir@hamptons.com
Website	www.southamptonhistoricalmuseum.com
When to Visit	Friday to Sunday
	2nd week of July to Columbus Day weekend
	11:00 a.m. to 5:00 p.m.
Charges/Fees	Adults—$3.00; seniors—$2.00; students—$1.00
Suggested Grades	4–Adult
Guided Tour	Yes
Maximum Group	40 (divided between exterior and interior)
Group Notice	2 weeks
Eating Facilities	Picnic in the orchard
Restroom Facilities	Yes
Handicapped Access	No

Walt Whitman Birthplace State Historic Site (c. 1819) and Interpretive Center

CONSTRUCTED OF HAND-HEWN beams and authentically furnished, the newly restored house is a fine example of native Long Island craftsmanship. The new Interpretive Center exhibits trace the poet's development from his boyhood on Long Island to his international prominence as one of our country's greatest visionaries. The exhibits include over 130 portraits of Walt Whitman, as well as original letters, manuscripts, artifacts and a schoolmaster's desk. The Interpretive Center also houses a library, museum shop and bookstore, a multimedia area including a "Seek and Find" interactive available for children, a video and Whitman's voice on tape, and a large meeting room.

Address/Telephone 246 Old Walt Whitman Road
South Huntington, NY 11746
(631) 427-5240

When to Visit Winter hours:
Wednesday to Friday—1:00 p.m. to 4:00 p.m.
Saturday and Sunday—11:00 a.m. to 4:00 p.m.
Closed major holidays.
Summer hours:
Monday and Wednesday to Friday—
11:00 a.m. to 4:00 p.m.
Saturday and Sunday—12:00 p.m. to 5:00 p.m.
Closed Tuesdays and major holidays.

Charges/Fees Adults—$3.00; seniors and students—
$2.00; children (7–12)—$1.00; children under 6—free

Suggested Grades 2–Adult

Guided Tour Yes

Maximum Group 48, with adequate supervision

Group Notice 2 weeks

Eating Facilities Picnic facilities on premises and restaurants nearby

Restroom Facilities Yes

Handicapped Access Yes

Additional Information Video program.
Museum shop and bookstore.
Auto-hiking tours of West Hills, including Jayne's Hill, Long Island's highest point.

Custer Institute

THE INSTITUTE HAS an astronomical observatory containing 10" refracting binoculars, a 10" CCD capable reflector, a 6" Eichner refractor, a 5" Alvan Clark refractor, a 3-meter radio telescope, an auditorium, library, small museum, mirror-grinding workshop, optical shop, darkroom and exhibits. In addition to astronomy, programs include such topics as economics, philosophy, ecology, music and the arts. Some meetings are open to members only, but frequently the public is invited to an evening of stargazing or a program of classic films, concerts, art exhibits, etc. The observatory is open to the public most Saturday nights, weather permitting.

Address/Telephone	P.O. Box 1204 Main Bay View Road Southold, NY 11971 (631) 765-2626
When to Visit	Call (631) 722-3850 or (631) 218-2350 for appointment
Charges/Fees	Donation
Suggested Grades	7–Adult
Guided Tour	Yes, up to 2 hours, by appointment
Maximum Group	30
Group Notice	2 weeks
Eating Facilities	Picnic facilities
Restroom Facilities	Yes
Handicapped Access	No
Additional Information	Write for most recent schedule of programs and activities: Barbara Lebkuecher, Treas., Herricks Lane, Box 645, Jamesport, NY 11947

Horton Point Lighthouse
Marine Museum
(Southold Historical Society)

BUILT 1856, FIRST lit 1857. Its third-order light, moved to a skeletal structure in 1933, was returned to its tower and recommissioned by the U.S. Coast Guard in 1990. Overlooking Long Island Sound, the building and property, owned by Southold Park District, have been cooperatively restored with the Southold Historical Society, which operates the Marine Museum. Horton Point Lighthouse is the most accessible of the six lighthouses in the Town of Southold.

Address/Telephone Southold Historical Society
Lighthouse Road
Southold, NY 11971
(631) 765-5500 (weekdays, 9:30 a.m. to 2:30 p.m.)

Lighthouse
(631) 765-2101 (weekend hours)

When to Visit Saturday and Sunday
May 30 to October 12
11:30 a.m. to 4:00 p.m.

Charges/Fees Suggested donation—$2.00

Horton Point Lighthouse

VALENTINE RUCH

Suggested Grades 3–Adult

Guided Tour Yes, 30 minutes

Maximum Group 40, with adequate supervision

Group Notice 2 weeks

Eating Facilities Picnic facilities

Restroom Facilities Yes

Handicapped Access No

Additional Information Film-viewing room, outdoor concerts, etc. Please call for information.

Southold Historical Museum
(Southold Historical Society)

SOUTHOLD, FOUNDED IN 1640, was the first English-speaking settlement on Long Island. The Southold Historical Society operates a museum in which the main Victorian house contains an art gallery, a millinery room and a collection of dolls, toys and period furniture. Also on site are the Thomas Moore pre-Revolutionary house, the Pine Neck Barn, a carriage house, blacksmith shop, The Buttery, complete with utensils, and the Old Bayview Schoolhouse.

Address/Telephone Main Road and Maple Lane
Southold, NY 11971
(631) 765-5500

When to Visit Wednesday, Saturday and Sunday
July and August
1:00 p.m. to 4:00 p.m.

Charges/Fees Suggested donation—$2.00

Suggested Grades K–Adult

Guided Tour Yes, 1 hour

Maximum Group 30, with adequate supervision

Group Notice 2 weeks

Eating Facilities Picnic facilities nearby

Restroom Facilities Yes

Handicapped Access Yes

Additional Information Museum shop next block

Southold Indian Museum
(The Incorporated Long Island Chapter, New York State Archaeological Association)

THIS ARCHAEOLOGICAL MUSEUM houses one of the most complete collections of Algonquin artifacts to be found on Long Island. One exhibit displays the numerous varieties of corn grown by local Indians, another displays collections of spears and arrowheads. There is also the largest collection of restored Algonquin ceramic pottery. The museum collection contains over 300,000 artifacts (not all on display at one time).

Address/Telephone P.O. Box 268
1080 Main Bay View Road
Southold, NY 11971
(631) 765-5577
Email: indianmuseum@aol.com

When to Visit Saturday and Sunday (July, August)
1:30 p.m. to 4:30 p.m.
Groups by arrangement (Monday–Saturday)

Charges/Fees $2.00 admission

Suggested Grades Pre-K–Adult (special children's program for grades 2–5 in August). For more information ask for "Education News Notes."

Guided Tour Available upon request

Maximum Group 40 (By arrangement, larger groups can be accommodated)

Group Notice 2 weeks or more would be appreciated

Eating Facilities By arrangement

Restroom Facilities Yes

Handicapped Access No

Additional Information Museum Shop available.

Wicks Farm and Garden

G ROUPS ARE FREE to tour greenhouses that grow spring annuals. Festive seasons offer wide displays of goblins, witches, turkeys and other objects when appropriate. The most popular time for children at the Wicks Farm and Garden is during the Halloween pumpkin picking and witch and goblin time from mid-September through October 31st.

Address/Telephone	445 North Country Road (Route 25A)
	St. James, NY 11780
	(631) 584-5727
When to Visit	Halloween Season—September 15 to October 31
	10:00 a.m. to 5:00 p.m.
	Schools and groups: Call for appointment
Charges/Fees	Call for information
Suggested Grades	Pre-K–Adult
Guided Tour	None
Maximum Group	Unlimited
Group Notice	1 month
Eating Facilities	None
Restroom Facilities	Yes, portable
Handicapped Access	Yes
Additional Information	Festive seasons and holidays offer special displays.

Electronic Explorations:
The Salt Marsh Ecosystem

S TUDENTS WHO participate in this program can study a marine environment without ever leaving the classroom. This distance learning program utilizes two-way video conferencing and wireless technology to enable students outside our locale to "visit" and study the temperate salt marsh. With the help of a qualified naturalist, students explore the plants and animals native to the marsh and their respective roles in the marsh food web. Wearing a wireless camera set in a specially-equipped pair of eyeglasses, and a vest which transmits two-way audio, the naturalist teaches right from the water's edge. Students are able to see the live specimens the naturalist uncovers, ask questions and converse with him or her in real time.

Address/Telephone	The Ward Melville Heritage Organization
	P.O. Box 572
	Stony Brook, NY 11790
	(631) 751-2244
Website	www.wardmelvilleheritage.org
When to Visit	Year-round by appointment
Charges/Fees	$125.00 for remote class
	$8.00 per person for on-site class
Suggested Grades	Can be tailored to appropriate grade levels
Guided Tour	Yes, approximately 1 hour for remote class;
	2 hours for on-site students
Maximum Group	25 (on-site class)
Group Notice	Call for information
Eating Facilities	Yes
Restroom Facilities	Yes
Handicapped Access	Yes
Additional Information	This program is broadcast from the Marine Conservation Center. Remote students connect with the naturalist in the wetlands, or remote students connect with the naturalist and a local class on-site in the wetlands. Call for more information.

Fresh Water Pond Ecology
at the Stony Brook Mill Pond

THIS PROGRAM provides students with the diversified spectrum of the fresh water pond ecology system. Students observe and explore the pond food web and its link to energy. Characteristics of aquatic plant life, pond creatures that live in fresh water, water quality, surface animals and other insects will be investigated. A scenic, informative nature trail accompanies the program. It includes the fascinating habitat where cormorants, egrets, mallards, Canada geese and other wildlife reside. Students experience an in-depth look at pond ecology while simultaneously discovering the delights of a pond trip.

Address/Telephone Harbor Road, off Main Street
Stony Brook, NY
For reservations:
The Ward Melville Heritage Organization
P.O. Box 572
Stony Brook, NY 11790
(631) 751-2244

Website www.wardmelvilleheritage.org

When to Visit March to December
Call for reservations.

Charges/Fees $5.00 per person (adults included/teacher exempt)
$60.00 minimum

Suggested Grades Can be tailored to appropriate grade levels

Guided Tour Yes, 1 hour

Maximum Group 30

Group Notice Call for information

Eating Facilities Yes

Restroom Facilities Yes

Handicapped Access Yes

The Long Island Museum of American Art, History & Carriages

VISITORS CAN enjoy art exhibitions from the museum's permanent collection as well as traveling exhibitions from America's leading artists and art institutions. The Long Island Museum is home to the nation's largest carriage collection, and over 100 carriages are always on view. The Margaret M. Blackwell History Museum hosts dynamic exhibitions

exploring cultural and social themes. It houses a gallery of fifteen miniature rooms and one of the top hand-carved antique duck decoy collections
in the United States. Public programs, children's summer programs and
other events are hosted regularly at the museum.

Address/Telephone 1200 Route 25A
Stony Brook, NY 11790
(631) 751-0066

Website www.longislandmuseum.org

When to Visit Wednesday to Saturday and most Monday
holidays—10:00 a.m. to 5:00 p.m.
Sunday—Noon to 5:00 p.m.
Open daily July and August

Charges/Fees Adults—$4.00; seniors—$3.00; children 6–18 and
students with I.D.—$2.00; museum members
and children under 6—free

Suggested Grades K–Adult

The Long Island Museum of American Art, History & Carriages

Guided Tour	Yes, call for special appointment
Maximum Group	35
Group Notice	2 weeks
Eating Facilities	Picnic facilities
Restroom Facilities	Yes
Handicapped Access	Yes
Additional Information	Special education programs available

Marine Conservation Center

LOCATED IN THE heart of The Ward Melville Heritage Organization's Wetlands Preserve, the Marine Conservation Center is an ideal location for students to learn about the environment. The Coastal Ecology program is offered in cooperation with Stony Brook University's Marine Sciences Research Center. Students learn the geology of Long Island and how the island was formed, how plants and animals live together in salt marsh habitats, and how Native Americans used the area's natural resources. The program also includes: a "touch tank" with shellfish, fin fish and plants; identification of the elements of a food web; and microscopic plants and animals projected onto a video microscope screen. Students then take a nature walk on the beach where they identify shells, rocks, marsh grasses and many other plants and animals.

Address/Telephone	The Ward Melville Heritage Organization P.O. Box 572 Stony Brook, NY 11790 (631) 751-2244
Website	www.wardmelvilleheritage.org
When to Visit	Year-round by appointment
Charges/Fees	$5.00 per student with a minimum of $80
Suggested Grades	Can be tailored to appropriate grade levels
Guided Tour	Yes
Maximum Group	30
Group Notice	Call for information on group programs.
Eating Facilities	Yes
Restroom Facilities	Yes
Handicapped Access	Yes

Museum of Long Island Natural Sciences

L OCATED IN THE Earth and Space Sciences Building, the Museum of Long Island Natural Sciences is dedicated to preserving and interpreting the natural heritage of Long Island. With a 20-year distinguished history, the Museum offers multifaceted opportunities for environmental education through its exhibits, publications, films, lectures, seminars and educational programs. The exhibit areas feature both changing exhibits and a permanent exhibit on Long Island Geology.

Address/Telephone	Earth and Space Sciences Building SUNY at Stony Brook Stony Brook, NY 11794-2100 (631) 632-8230 Fax: (631) 632-8240
Website	www.molins.sunysb.edu
When to Visit	Monday to Friday—9:00 a.m. to 5:00 p.m.
Charges/Fees	None. Small fee for programs.
Suggested Grades	Pre-K–Adult
Guided Tour	None
Maximum Group	60
Group Notice	Advance reservations
Eating Facilities	Available on campus
Restroom Facilities	Yes
Handicapped Access	Yes

Pontoon "Discovery" Wetlands Cruise

T HE "DISCOVERY" CRUISE provides a unique field trip in environmental ecology guided by a qualified naturalist from Stony Brook University's Marine Sciences Research Center. Students board the pontoon boat for a cruise from Stony Brook Harbor into the surrounding wetlands. Close-up views of the moraine, the tidal flow, grasses and birds are enhanced by a lively interactive discussion involving the history of the area. The students are invited to "experience" the wetlands using all of their senses. With

their eyes closed they are asked to identify the various sounds of the wetlands. Sample marine specimens and hands-on activities such as Bird
Bingo help the students to identify the wildlife they see. Shipbuilding and
the history of various homes along the shores are also discussed.

Address/Telephone	The Ward Melville Heritage Organization P.O. Box 572 Stony Brook, NY 11790 (631) 751-2244
Website	www.wardmelvilleheritage.org
When to Visit	May through October
Charges/Fees	Individual rate for open boat days: Adults—$15.00; children under 12—$9.00. Group rate: Adult groups—$420.00; school groups—$250.00.
Suggested Grades	Program can be tailored to appropriate grade levels
Guided Tour	Yes
Maximum Group	35 passengers
Group Notice	Call for information
Eating Facilities	Yes, nearby
Restroom Facilities	Yes
Handicapped Access	Limited
Additional Information	Reservations required for group tours.

Staller Center for the Arts
(Stony Brook University)

WITH ITS FIVE theaters and 4,700-square-foot art gallery, Staller Center
is the only comprehensive center for the arts of Long Island. The
Center is open year-round and offers world-class attractions in music,
film, ballet, theater, the visual arts and lectures. In the summer it is the
venue for the Stony Brook Film Festival.

Address/Telephone	Stony Brook, NY 11794
	(631) 632-7235 (tours)
	(631) 632-ARTS (ticket/performance information)
When to Visit	Call or write for schedule
Charges/Fees	Varies with program
Suggested Grades	All ages depending on program
Guided Tour	By special arrangement only
Maximum Group	Varies with program
Group Notice	2 weeks
Eating Facilities	Yes
Restroom Facilities	Yes
Handicapped Access	Yes
Additional Information	Many performances free or voluntary donation

Stony Brook Grist Mill

OWNED AND OPERATED by The Ward Melville Heritage Organization, the Stony Brook Grist Mill, c. 1751, is Long Island's most completely equipped working grist mill. It is operated by a miller as it was in the 18th and 19th centuries. The water-powered, overshot mill is listed on the National Register of Historic Places as a rare example of Dutch framing. Students experience milling firsthand in this program taught by a qualified instructor. They shell corn, bag ground grain, feed cracked corn to the ducks at the adjacent mill pond, and earn "Dusty" certificates as assistant millers.

Address/Telephone	The Ward Melville Heritage Organization
	P.O. Box 572
	Stony Brook, NY 11790
	(631) 751-2244
Website	www.wardmelvilleheritage.org

When to Visit	General public: June to September Wednesday to Sunday—Noon to 4:30 p.m. April, May, October and November Saturday and Sunday—Noon to 4:30 p.m. "Dusty program": March to December
Charges/Fees	Individual tours: Adults—$2.00; children under 12—$1.00. (Educational program is $5.00 per person.) Group adult tours also available by appointment.
Suggested Grades	All ages, depending on the program
Guided Tour	Yes, groups by arrangement
Maximum Group	Can accommodate groups of 30
Group Notice	Call in advance for group reservations.
Eating Facilities	Yes, nearby
Restroom Facilities	Yes
Handicapped Access	Yes, but limited—higher floors available by video.
Additional Information	"Dusty program"—Pre-trip educational kit available for teachers.

University Art Gallery—
Staller Center for the Arts
(Stony Brook University)

THE UNIVERSITY ART GALLERY, located in the Staller Center for the Arts at Stony Brook University, is a double-storied, 4,700-square-foot facility with 200 running feet of wall space. The gallery presents five exhibitions of contemporary art each year.

Address/Telephone	Stony Brook, NY 11794-5425 (631) 632-7240

When to Visit Tuesday to Friday—Noon to 4:00 p.m.
Saturday—6:00 p.m. to 8:00 p.m.
Also open to the public prior to some evening
performances at the Staller Center for the Arts.

Charges/Fees None

Suggested Grades High school to Adult

Guided Tour By arrangement

Maximum Group 20

Group Notice 2 weeks

Eating Facilities Yes, at cafeterias in other locations on campus

Restroom Facilities Yes

Handicapped Access Yes

Brookhaven National Laboratory

EXPLORE THE MARVELS of science and learn about Brookhaven National Laboratory; tours, audio-visual presentations, school programs and special events.

Address/Telephone Community, Education, Government
& Public Affairs Office
35 Brookhaven Avenue, Bldg. 134
Upton, NY 11973
(631) 344-2345

Website www.bnl.gov

When to Visit Summer Sundays—July 14 to August 25
10:00 a.m. to 3:00 p.m.
Schools and groups: programs by appointment
(year-round)

Charges/Fees None

Suggested Grades	K–Adult
Guided Tour	Yes, length depends on program
Maximum Group	By arrangement
Group Notice	3 weeks
Eating Facilities	Cafeteria
Restroom Facilities	Yes
Handicapped Access	Yes
Additional Information	All visitors age 15 and over must bring a photo ID to enter the Laboratory site.

Duck Walk Vineyards

EXPERIENCE AWARD-WINNING wines in an extraordinary French Normandy château. The winery is situated on 40 acres of vineyards and features tours and tastings daily. Learn about the centuries-old process of winemaking with state-of-the-art equipment. There is live music on Saturday and Sunday afternoons from May to October.

Address/Telephone	231 Montauk Highway Water Mill, NY 11976 (631) 726-7555
Website	www.duckwalk.com
When to Visit	Daily Year-round 11:00 a.m. to 6:00 p.m. for tours and wine tasting
Charges/Fees	None
Suggested Grades	K–Adult
Guided Tour	Yes, 30 minutes
Maximum Group	100
Group Notice	1 week

Eating Facilities Picnic facilities available

Restroom Facilities Yes

Handicapped Access Yes

Additional Information Call for special events and program calendar

Water Mill Museum

THIS GRISTMILL IS the oldest operating water mill on Long Island. Water-driven, it houses tools of a miller, cooper, carpenter, blacksmith, wheelwright, weaver and spinner. The exhibits encourage viewer participation—you may try the mortar and pestle, turn wooden gears and use a fanning mill. Art exhibits.

Address/Telephone *Old Mill Road (off Route 27)
Water Mill, NY 11976
(631) 726-4625

Website www.watermillmuseum.org

When to Visit May to September
Thursday to Monday—11:00 a.m. to 5:00 p.m.
Sunday—1:00 p.m. to 5:00 p.m.
Closed Tuesday and Wednesday
Groups by appointment

Charges/Fees Adults—$3.00; seniors—$2.00;
children and members—free

Suggested Grades K–Adult

Guided Tour Yes, 40 minutes

Maximum Group 40

Group Notice Call for information

Eating Facilities None

Restroom Facilities Yes

Handicapped Access First floor only

Additional Information Call in advance. School tours: Call above number
or (631) 283-7151.
*Mailing address: P.O. Box 63, Water Mill, NY
11976

Southwest Sewer District at Bergen Point

VISITORS WILL OBSERVE the largest water-treatment plant utilizing primary and secondary treatment of liquid sewage wastes in Suffolk County. It is designed to treat over 30 million gallons of waste water per day, producing a clear effluent free of harmful or objectionable materials and meeting all federal requirements. Other trips to facilities utilizing different processes at the University at Stony Brook and the County Centers at Hauppauge and Yaphank can also be arranged by calling (631) 852-4109.

Address/Telephone	600 Bergen Avenue
	West Babylon, NY 11704
	(631) 854-4150
When to Visit	Tuesday, Wednesday and Thursday
	April to September
	By appointment only—weather permitting
Charges/Fees	None
Suggested Grades	9–Adult
Guided Tour	Yes, 1 hour
Maximum Group	20, with one adult per group of 10
Group Notice	2 weeks
Eating Facilities	None
Restroom Facilities	Yes
Handicapped Access	No
Additional Information	By calling (631) 852-4109, visits to additional facilities (SUNY/Stony Brook, Yaphank, Hauppauge) with different processes can be arranged.

Sagtikos Manor

AT THE HOUSE, the original part of which was constructed in 1692, visitors will observe many items of historical significance. Furnishings and a style of living for the well-to-do during the Revolutionary period are available for study. The house was occupied by British General Sir Henry Clinton during the American Revolution and was included in the tour of Long Island by President Washington.

Sagtikos Manor

LOUIS DORMAND

Address/Telephone	*Montauk Highway West Bay Shore, NY 11706 (631) 661-8348
When to Visit	Call for information
Charges/Fees	Call for information
Suggested Grades	3–Adult
Guided Tour	Yes, approximately 45 minutes
Maximum Group	Call for information
Group Notice	Call for information
Eating Facilities	None
Restroom Facilities	Yes
Handicapped Access	No
Additional Information	At time of print, Sagtikos Manor was temporarily closed; will reopen shortly. Please call for more information. *Mailing address: P.O. Box P344, Bay Shore, NY 11706

Long Island Maritime Museum   MITCH CARUCCI

Long Island Maritime Museum

S TEP BACK IN time and appreciate the maritime history of Long Island while enjoying a panoramic view of the Great South Bay. The museum contains a main exhibition hall with changing exhibits, a fully restored 19th-century Bayman's Cottage, two Long Island-built oystering vessels docked next to the historic Oyster Cull House, and a working Boatshop. The museum's educational programs are committed to providing students with an integrated look into Long Island's natural and ethnic history.

Address/Telephone P.O. Box 184
86 West Avenue
West Sayville, NY 11796
(631) HIS-TORY, (631) 854-4974
Fax: (631) 854-4979
Email: limaritimemuseum@aol.com

Website www.limaritime.org

When to Visit Fall, Spring and Summer by appointment

Charges/Fees Adults—$4.00; seniors and children—$2.00
Group tours: $4.00 per student; no charge for
accompanying adults

Suggested Grades 4–11

Guided Tour Yes

Maximum Group 75

Group Notice 2 weeks minimum

Eating Facilities "Brown bag"

Restroom Facilities Yes

Handicapped Access Yes

Additional Information The museum provides comprehensive pre-trip materials and evaluation tools. Please call for specialized tours, or with any special needs.

Suffolk County Farm and Education Center

THE SUFFOLK COUNTY Farm and Education Center, managed by Cornell Cooperative Extension of Suffolk County, offers a unique opportunity for families and groups to see a real working farm with cattle, pigs, hens, turkeys and other domesticated animals, and a historic haybarn built in 1871.

Address/Telephone *Yaphank Avenue
Yaphank, NY 11980
(631) 852-4600

Website www.cce.cornell.edu/suffolk

When to Visit Daily
9:00 a.m. to 3:00 p.m.
Gift shop hours: call (631) 852-4608

Charges/Fees Public—free; groups—by arrangement

Suggested Grades Pre-K–Adult

Guided Tour Yes, by appointment

Maximum Group By arrangement

Group Notice 1 month—general public needs no reservations

Eating Facilities Picnic facilities available

Restroom Facilities Yes

Handicapped Access Yes (Note: there are dirt roads.)

Additional Information Call for information on workshops, classes, educational programs and special events. No dogs allowed.
*Mailing address: P.O. Box 129, Yaphank, NY 11980-0129

CATEGORY INDEX

MISCELLANEOUS

NATURE, SCIENCE AND ECOLOGY

ALPHABETICAL INDEX

This is a strict alphabetization by exact full title of facility
(only opening "The's" are omitted).